Carver's Manual
on
Community Theatre
Directing

(A STEP-BY-STEP APPROACH)

by

James Carver

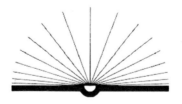

Hansa-Hewlett Publishing Company LLC

Kalamazoo, Michigan USA

Carver, James C.
  Carver's Manual on Community Theatre Directing:
  A Step-by-Step Approach/ James C. Carver.—1st ed.

  Includes bibliographical references.

      ISBN: 978-0-945732-08-2
      Library of Congress Control Number: 2010922971

Published by Hansa-Hewlett Publishing Company LLC
Kalamazoo, Michigan
www.Hansa-Hewlett.com

DEDICATION

This book is dedicated to my lovely wife, Nancy, who has always be-
lieved in me. Without her support and encouragement (i.e., pushing), this book would never have been written.

Give 'em your best!

Jim Carmony

ACKNOWLEDGMENTS

Thanks to those who helped

I am grateful to the following friends who read the manuscript in its early stages and offered insight, suggestions, and encouragement: Sharon Kirby Cole, Morrie Enders, Michael Ray Helms, David Oosting, Carl Beery Moore and Jane Moore; and to Diana Miller for her editing

CONTENTS

INTRODUCTION   10

ABOUT THE AUTHOR   11

PREFACE   12

CHAPTER 1 Getting Started   14

    Deciding What Kind of Play It Is—15

    Presentational or Representational—17

    The Circumstances of the Play—19

    The Arc of the Play—21

    Preparing the Production Concept—24

CHAPTER 2 Blocking   27

    Telling the Story Through Blocking—27

    Blocking Notations—37

CHAPTER 3 Auditioning Actors   40

    Director Preparation—40

    Preparing the Actors for the Audition—42

    The Audition—45

    Callbacks—47

CHAPTER 4 Rehearsals   51

    The Rehearsal Schedule—51

    Preparing the Rehearsal Schedule—53

The First Rehearsal—55

Administrative Issues—56

Sharing the Artistic Vision—57

The First Read-Through—57

Blocking Rehearsals—58

Working Rehearsals—61

When to Start "No Books"—63

When to Start Using Props—63

Run-Through Week—64

The First Technical Rehearsal—65

Opening Night—70

CHAPTER 5 Directing the Actor   **71**

Directing the Inexperienced Actor—72

Creating a Character—72

Creating the Character's Thinking—77

Visualization—79

Natural Speech—81

Speaking All the Way to the End of the Line—82

Eliminating Punctuation—82

Our "Bag of Words"—83

Finding the Important Words—83

Talking "To" Not "At"—84

"Mary Had a Little Lamb" Exercise—85

The "What?" Exercise—86

Listen!—86

The Head Voice—87

The Half Voice—88

The Actor's Body—88

Some General Notes on Dealing with Actors—90

CHAPTER 6 Directing Comedy   93

Deciding What's Funny—94

The Mechanics of Comedy—96

Styles of Comedy —98

Slapstick—98

Farce—99

British Farce—101

French Farce—102

Gag Comedy—102

Situation Comedy—102

Sophisticated Comedy—103

Comedy of Manners—104

Restoration Comedy—105

The Comedy of Moliere—106

Satire—106

Playing Honestly—108

Permission to Laugh—109

Basic Elements of Playing Comedy—110

Pace—110

Timing —116

Focus—120

Delivery—121

The Actor's Body—123

"Takes" —124

Holding for Laughs—126

CHAPTER 7 Directing Drama   129

The Importance of the Story—130

Tools to Tell the Story—131

The Importance of the Characters—135

The Struggle—136

Audience Involvement—137

Playing the End of the Play Too Soon—139

Hole Fixing—139

Rhythm, Tempo and Pace—141

CHAPTER 8 Directing Musicals   145

Organization, Organization, Organization—148

Working With the Musical Director and
  the Choreographer—153

Staging Musical Numbers—160

Technical Considerations—166

Scene Changes—166

The Follow Spot—169

Lighting —170

To Mic or Not to Mic—171

Putting It All Together—171

AFTERWORD "If It Ain't Fun, It Ain't Worth It"   177

"Give 'Em Your Best"—178

Community Theatre: Our National Theatre—179

REFERENCES   180

Plays Quoted from or Referred to—180

Books Quoted from or Referred to—184

INTRODUCTION

James Carver set out to write a "How To" book for those interested in directing at community theatres. He has succeeded in doing much more than writing a manual. He has written a *Chautauqua, an anecdotal instruction book for all aspiring actors, directors, producers and managers in a witty and enlightening manner— and above all, a book for those who love the magic of community theatre, and are fascinated by what "goes on behind the scenes."

Nor should the lessons of this manual be limited to community theatre. The principles so clearly enunciated apply to all theatre productions, certainly to theatre at the high school and college level; and neither should any professional director, no matter what may be his or her skills or level of achievement, be without this manual. The basics are presented in an unforgettable manner, and "why didn't I think of that," pops up on every other page.

The editors
Hansa-Hewlett Publishing Company

*Chautauqua (from a lake in western New York): an institution that flourished in the late 19th and early 20th Centuries providing popular education combined with entertainment in the form of lectures, concerts, and plays often presented outdoors in a tent.

About the Author

James Carver (Jim, please) is a third generation theatre professional. His grandparents and his mother toured the United States during the early 1900s. His grandfather, though never famous, was an actor whom every everyone in show business knew and respected. When Jim's mother and father were married they settled in Kalamazoo, Michigan, where there was a professional theatre company. In 1929, they helped found the Kalamazoo Civic Players which became one of the premier community theatres in the country. (During WWII the Players were invited to take a production to Broadway.) In the early 30s the beautiful and state-of-the-art Civic Auditorium was built and became the home of the Players.

Jim was literally born back stage. His earliest memories of theatre come from watching his parents in hundreds of rehearsals and performances. He claims to have learned his craft by osmosis from the back row of the theatre where his parents propped him up in a seat while they rehearsed. As he grew older he participated as an actor in the theatre's children's program. He was educated at Michigan State University, earning Bachelor and Masters degrees. Jim joined the professional staff of the Kalamazoo Civic Players in 1958 as a production assistant—building, painting, teaching and directing. In 1967 He took over the reins of the theatre from his retiring father. In 1974, he was named the Managing Director, which included the duties of Artistic Director. Under Jim's guidance the Kalamazoo Civic grew to be one of the largest in the country, presenting twenty two productions each year with eight hundred volunteers and a professional staff of seventeen.

Carver has directed hundreds of plays and has acted in as many roles. He has developed an international reputation as a director: two of his productions were selected in national competition to represent the United States at international festivals, the most recent being *Dancing at Lughnasa* at the World Amateur Theatre Festival in Monaco. The judges at that festival called the production "the finest that had ever represented the United States." Jim has adjudicated countless American Association of Community Theatre festivals, including twice at the national. He is in constant demand as a workshop leader. Jim has served as President of AACT and from that group has received its highest award for a lifetime of leadership in community theatre. He presently lives in Colorado and directs for community theatres nationwide.

PREFACE

A few years ago I was attending a workshop on directing at a national theatre convention. I always want to hear other director's thoughts on directing, because I steal anything that works. This leader of the workshop sat on the table in front of us all and proceeded to tell anecdote after anecdote—just stories about his experiences in directing: "Oh, I had trouble with this actor," giving us all the details about this run-in with someone we neither knew nor cared about. The anecdotes were endless. All the directors taking this workshop were growing restless. There was nothing to be learned. I couldn't stand it any longer, so I asked a question: "Do you think a director should also be a teacher?" He narrowed his eyes and looked at me as if to say, "How dare you ask such a question and interrupt my telling you what a wonderful person I am?" He answered my question with a few words and then launched into another hilarious (to him) anecdote. Slowly the room began to empty. A few of us decided to stick it out.

As I walked out the door at the conclusion, I said to one of my fellow suffering participants, "Well, that certainly was a waste of time." She turned to me and said, "You know, I have been in many of your workshops on acting and directing. You should write a book on directing in community theatre." I said, "Have you been talking to my wife?"

There are a lot of books on directing. Some are great—a must-read—some are OK in that the author gives you the basics, and some are just plain awful and should replace the Sears catalog in the outhouse. None of these books, great to awful, addresses the subject of directing in community theatre, which is a whole different animal than directing in professional or educational theatre. Can you imagine a professional director having to cast the only three men that showed up at auditions, none of whom is right for any of the three male roles, and having to say, "Well, maybe I can make it work"? We do this all the time. It's what community theatre is all about—taking what we have to work with and doing the best we can.

I have spent my whole life working in community theatre. Most of that time I have been a paid professional, but some of the time I have been a volunteer. I don't know how many plays I've directed or how many roles I've played. I don't keep track of things like that. The next project is what is important, not the last one. At any rate, I have learned a lot about directing in community theatre in the last forty-five years. And I believe in community theatre so strongly that I want everyone to love and enjoy it as much as I do. I want everyone to do the best they can do. One of the things we face in community theatre is that most of the people who come to us have talent, but no craft. They have the spirit, the imagination, and the desire, but they don't have the training or the tools to do their best work. That's why I do workshops. I certainly don't know everything about directing and acting, but what I have learned, I am eager to share. Much of what is in this book comes from my experiences in rehearsals and workshops.

So, what I'm going to do in this book is to share with you some of the methods I have developed and some of the solutions to problems I have found that face the director in community theatre. My basic approach will be to tell you what I do, not what you should do. You may know a lot of this from your previous work or study. If that's true, maybe I can just organize your thinking for you. Steal anything you want. Try it. Use it. If it doesn't work for you, then modify it so that it does or throw it away. Replace the Sears catalog in the outhouse with it if you feel like it. *THERE ARE NO RIGHTS OR WRONGS IN DIRECTING.*

CHAPTER ONE

GETTING STARTED

When I first pick up a play, knowing that I'm going to direct it, I make a lot of notes, in pencil in the inside margin. I'll tell you why the inside later. As I read, images go through my head. I may see a conversation taking place over a table—say, two people arguing and they are both leaning into each other and almost nose-to-nose. I note that. I may not be able to use that later, but that note reminds me of a relationship between those two people at that moment. I note anything that occurs to me as I read. I may see stage pictures; I may hear line readings; I may see colors; I may be reminded of something from my past; my mind may wander while I am reading, and I note that and also what it wanders to. If certain images keep coming up to me off the page, repetitively, I note that.

For instance, if I'm aware that there is a frequent reference to blood or death, or red, I note it. I'm interpreting the script, determining what the play is saying to me. I need to capture these thoughts so I can use them later when I get into full analysis of the play. Understand, I may discard many of these notes as meaningless and unusable, but at least they remind me of what I was thinking at the time of my first reading.

Let me say a few words about interpreting here. We all come to a play with different backgrounds and experiences. When we read something, it may give me one set of images and you a completely different set. There is an exercise that I do in one of my workshops where I have all the participants close their eyes and I ask them to capture the image that goes through their heads when I say one word. Then I say the word "mother." I give them a second and then call upon several individuals to tell us about their image.

There is an infinite variety. One may see a *Madonna and Child*. Another sees her mother, a short, round woman with a smiling face and wearing an apron. One person sees an older woman in a wheelchair suffering in pain. It goes on and on, each one different. Each person has interpreted the word "mother" from his or her own experience. As directors, we are going to interpret thousands of words. That's why my production of a play is going to be different from your production. We just don't share the same experiences and backgrounds. When we say we are going to direct a play, we take a silent oath that essentially says, "Given my available talent and resources, I will faithfully produce this play as the author intended." No way! What we really are doing is producing it to say what it had to say to us. "Sorry, author. I think this is what you were trying to say. I may not be right, but I'm not wrong."

A final word about note taking: When I am finished reading the play, I go back and read all my marginal notes. I look for patterns and repeated images. Is there a key phrase that describes what this play says to me? Sometimes yes, sometimes no. Even if the answer is no, I have a fairly good place to start my analysis of the play.

Deciding What Kind of Play It Is

I find it important to decide what kind of play I'm dealing with. Two major questions right off the bat are: Is it a comedy or is it a drama? If it's a comedy, what kind is it? There are lots of different kinds of comedy. *Noises Off*, which requires a lot of physical humor and a breakneck pace, is not the same kind of comedy as *Private Lives* which requires style, grace, and ease. So I need to decide what makes this play funny. Is it the action? The situation? The characters? The language? I'm very fond of saying, "If the curtain goes up and there are six doors on the set—it's a farce." Why? Because lots of people are going to be running in and out of and slamming those doors. The action is going to be fast and furious. If we tried to do Noel Coward's *Private Lives* in the same way, we would make a major blunder. The action in the latter play is not what is important. It's the language, the characters, and the living style of those people that we laugh at. Neil Simon's *Barefoot In The Park* is funny, not for the language, not for the characters, not for the action. It's funny because of the situation. A newlywed couple moves into an apartment that is six floors up (if you don't count the stoop). It's a small apartment; they can hardly get into the bedroom; there's a hole in the skylight; there is a strange man living above them; her mother insists on visiting them unannounced. It's the situation that's funny. So, you don't try to make language funny; you don't try to make the characters funny. You concentrate on the situation. The only reason the telephone man and the delivery man are funny is because of the situation. If this apartment was on the first floor, these characters would lose their humor. When it snows through the broken skylight, we laugh because of the situation. And why do we laugh? Because it is serious to those people onstage.

There is a lot of literature out there about drama types and styles. Since I'm not a theatre scholar—I'm a practitioner—I'm not going to attempt to discuss all the different styles of dramatic literature as they relate to a director. If I have a feel for the general kind of play I'm working on, I'll go to a scholarly source book to read about that particular type. For instance, what makes a true "tragedy," in the classical sense, as opposed to a "drama"? What are those elements? If I'm going to decide the nature of the beast I'm working on, I need to know as much about it as possible. For instance, we use the term "melodrama" a lot to describe certain kinds of plays. Some may confuse "melodrama" with "mellerdrama" and think that it means those overdone stagings of plays where the damsel is in distress, the young hero saves her from the clutches of the dastardly villain, and the audience cheers and throws popcorn. "Mellerdrama" certainly has elements of "melodrama." That's how it got its name. But the two must be played entirely differently.

Reading about "melodrama" can help define its elements and lead to the use of tools that enhance those elements. For instance, do I underscore a dramatic scene with creepy music to heighten the emotions being expressed? Do I light it so that there are lots of shadows and dark places? Do the doors creak when they are opened? Does a wolf howl in the night? Do we need to see the doorknob slowly turn? Do headlights from a car suddenly blaze in the darkened room? I realize I'm only talking about a particular kind of melodrama, but if I'm doing a play like *Night Must Fall*, a scary, creepy suspense drama, I need to know what tools to use to make it scary, creepy, and suspenseful.

Presentational or Representational?

One of the major decisions I have to make about what kind of play I'm dealing with is whether it is *presentational* or *representational*. Am I dealing with a play in which the audience is aware that the actors are performing for them? Do the characters involve them in the action? Do the characters talk directly to the audience? Do they make comments to and share thoughts with the audience? In other words, are they "presenting" a play for the audience? If there is a narrator, or a character such as in *Dancing At Lughnasa* or *Our Town,* one who starts the story and introduces us to parts of the action, then I am dealing with a *presentational* type of play. If the play is written in such a manner that the characters seem unaware of the audience's presence, if it seems we are watching the action through a tiny window in the "fourth wall" of the world inhabited by the characters, then we are probably dealing with a *representational* type of play. The author wants us to see a representation of real life. *Death Of A Salesman* would be such a play.

Why is this important? It affects a number of things in the way in which I prepare my production: from lighting to scenery to blocking (character movement.) For instance, in the play *Wit*, the lead character enters talking directly to the audience. She tells us who she is and what the situation is. The set has a hospital bed, not a complete hospital room, and stage areas are used to indicate different locations: an X -ray lab, a classroom, etc. Other set pieces are merely background for the action and masking (scenic units to hide back -stage.) I need to plan the characters' movements so that the lead comes forward to talk to the audience (when she can) or from her hospital bed (when she must); I need to design the lighting so that these "other locations" are lit when they are used; and I need to design the background units to be "anywhere." In the final scene I can have a special lighting effect to emphasize her death. All this fits well into the style of presentational—presenting her story.

Earlier I mentioned *Barefoot In The Park*. Nowhere in the play does a character talk directly to the audience. We see an apartment in New York in all its details. The apartment is lit as though there were lighting sources, that is, lamps, sconces, etc. Since we are looking at a representation of real life it would not be appropriate for characters to speak directly to the audience. If, as the director, I want a speech said straight front, I had better establish by lighting or action that there is a window downstage and the character is looking out the window as he or she speaks. Otherwise, the characters should be talking to each other to give the sense of reality. I must say, over the years I have seen this mistake made again and again: actors standing facing straight front addressing other actors, and directors bringing a character down center in a special light for "the big speech."

The Circumstances of the Play

As I continue my study of the play, I concern myself with the circumstances. I need to understand the world of the characters. The period of the play is important. For example, societal issues are completely different from era to era as we travel through time. Just look at the world at the beginning of the twentieth century and the beginning of the twenty-first. Morality, lifestyles, world situation, and political situation are all different. Even within the past century things changed drastically. The domestic comedies and dramas of the fifties have little in common with the struggle-for -self-expression plays of the sixties. The point is, that when I can place the time of the play, I need to understand the world at that time so that I know what the characters are dealing with.

If I'm doing one of Shakespeare's plays, I may want to examine the play to discover if there are any strong political or moral issues present that may be better understood by today's audiences if placed in a different time period or different location. Would *Romeo and Juliet* help the audience realize how relevant this play is now if it were presented as today in a gang-related ghetto? (Wait a minute, isn't that *West Side Story*?) Even though I might consider doing something like that, I do not ascribe to the "Wouldn't It Be Fun, Just for a Change, School of Directing." Helping the audience "get" the play is what is of importance, not dazzling them with my directorial brilliance.

Where does this play take place? A play set in Brooklyn means the characters have to deal with a world that is completely different from one set in west Texas. Not just speech patterns, but daily life. Many people in Brooklyn don't own a car—unthinkable in Texas where it is not unusual for them to drive a hundred miles to see a movie. Once I know the location of the play, I had better find out all about that world.

Other circumstances include the relationships of the characters. Married? Divorced? Interested in each other? Those things will be fairly obvious. However, a play is about conflict. I need to understand what each of the characters wants, their *super objective,* and what prevents them from achieving that objective. What a character wants and what prevents him from getting there will determine his actions. What obstacle must he overcome? In order to understand what a character wants, it may be necessary to look at his actions first. It's fairly easy to understand that Macbeth takes certain actions because he wants to be king. It may be a little more difficult to say what Willy Loman, in *Death of a Salesman*, wants by the actions he takes, but what he wants causes him to take certain actions. And the determination of objective, obstacle, and action is not limited to the lead characters. Every character, even the maid who enters and says "tea is served, mum" and exits, has as much of a life as the other characters. (I'll discuss this in more detail when I get to "Directing the Inexperienced Actor".) As a director, I need to know all this so that I can understand relationships. This understanding leads to an analysis of the function of each character. How does each character help tell the story? And when I understand the character's functions, motives, actions, and relationships, I can plan such things as blocking, focus, pacing, intensity, business, scenery, costuming, lighting, etc.

Two directors I admire, Jon Jory and Harold Clurman, say they read the play through from the perspective of each character. I have used that approach and it can give great insight into the characters.

One of the things I have done to help me (and the actors) to understand relationships among the characters is to diagram them. Just a simple diagram in which each character is represented by a circle with their initial in it. Then I draw an arrow from each character to every other character, and on that arrow shaft I comment on their relationship. Not detailed; just a phrase: "doesn't trust him," "loves her," etc. Understand, there are two arrows going between two characters: one might say "loves her" and the one coming from her might say "can't stand him."

The Arc of the Play

This term, *Arc*, sounds awfully academic and difficult. But it is really useful and easy to understand. In simple terms it means, how are things different at the end of the play than at the beginning? How did the conflict get resolved? Did the central character get what he wanted? If so, what is the situation? If not, what is the situation? It can't be the same as at the beginning. The characters' world has changed because of what they've been through. (If it is the same, why would an audience sit through the struggle to see no resolution?)

So I start with the circumstances at the beginning of the play, looking at all the facts. Macbeth (the character) is a war hero happy to be returning home from battle. That's it! But wait! Three witches he meets plant the idea that he may become king. All very well and good, except that there already is a king. Macbeth doesn't put much stock in the witches' words and essentially dismisses the idea. Now events seem to happen at a rapid pace. The king decides to visit Macbeth's castle and Macbeth's wife, having heard of the witches' prediction, says to her husband, "Hey, let's do this. If we do him in, you'll be king." Macbeth is reluctant, but she is determined. They do the deed and from there on it's downhill for Macbeth. Yeah, he's king alright, but he suddenly has ghosts visiting him; he has to plot the murders of others; he has to kill some innocent women and children; his wife dies; he has to summon his army to defend himself against his enemies; and, in the ultimate battle, Macbeth dies. So. How are things different at the end of the play from the beginning? There is the arc. (It also demonstrates the theme of the play: blind ambition leads to self-destruction.).

In the play I'm working on, I try to find ten to twelve events in the play that tell the whole story. These I refer to as *storytelling moments*. From the beginning to the end, there are several things that happen in the course of this play that really tell the whole story. If I were going to tell someone the story of Macbeth, I would not need much more than what was just outlined. Those are the storytelling moments. OK, why is this important? Well, we're storytellers. We want our listeners to "get" the story. So we make sure at every junction, every storytelling moment, that they are understanding what's going on. If we told the Macbeth story and paid little attention to the witches or Lady Macbeth, our audience would have a hard time understanding why all this was happening. These moments are important to the story. So we make them important in the production. We give them special attention. When we see Macbeth reluctant to commit murder, it is important that we see Lady Macbeth steel him to the task. In that moment, an important part of the story is being told. It needs special attention. In what way? Any way we can: lighting, blocking, focus, intensity, position on the stage, etc. We do it so the audience "gets it." And then we move on, preparing for the next *storytelling moment*. We certainly don't ignore everything between these moments, we merely ensure that these moments are crystal clear for the audience. The porter of the gate scene in *Macbeth* is a great comic scene providing some comic relief in the middle of a murderous night, and we want to give it its due, but in terms of advancing the story of Macbeth, it has little importance.

In order to completely understand the story, I say to myself (or write it down), this happened, then this happened, then this, then this. The story has finally reached a point where some major event happens that determines the outcome of the story. Does our hero win or lose? Where is it that Macbeth's fate is sealed? If you think of the arc like a curved line that rises and falls, then this major event is the top of the curve and the storytelling moments after that are leading us to the resolution.

OK, *Macbeth* is easy. What about a play like *Over the River and Through the Woods?* What are the storytelling moments that create the arc of that play? What starts the action of the play is the announcement of the grandson that he has been offered a job that will take him out of the city, leaving behind his devoted grandparents. The announcement is *storytelling moment* number one. The grandson and the grandparents struggle with this problem, creating more storytelling moments, until a scene on the porch with one of his grandparents where he receives a "blessing" on his decision to move. A big storytelling moment. The arc: Everything is great in the beginning until the announcement of the promotion; the grandparents try several things to get him to change his mind about accepting this job; he becomes ill trying to decide; he could decide not to take the job to appease his grandparents; and finally, one of his grandparents understands what it means to him and says "OK, then." And at the end of the play he has moved and the remaining grandmother has accepted the change and everything is "great" again. I've oversimplified this story, I know. But the fact remains that the situation at the end of the play is different than at the beginning and a number of events have occurred to make it different.

These events are the storytelling moments and need our special attention. Look at the scene on the porch when the grandfather finally understands why it is important to his grandson to accept this position and move away. Say the porch is extreme stage left; the two men go out on the porch to have this conversation. A choice has to be made by the director about who is going to be stage right (on the porch) and who is left. Who has the most important speech in the scene? The grandfather. If it is blocked so that the grandfather is stage right speaking to his grandson stage left, the speech is said into the wings and the focus is on the listener and not the speaker. Is the listener's reaction more important than what is being said? I think not. If the grandfather is blocked to be stage left, facing back onto the stage, we can focus on him, especially if we ask the actor playing the grandson to remain very still during this scene. All the focus goes to the grandfather for "the speech," and the audience "gets it." Add in the fact that the porch light is on the grandfather's face and on the grandson's back and you can see what I mean about paying special attention to storytelling moments and using all your tools.

Preparing the Production Concept

I've decided what the play is about—what it says to me. I must now find all the tools to tell this story to the audience. A novel writer has only the words he chooses; a painter has only the canvas and the paint; a musician has only the notes he writes and the instruments he selects. We have all of those tools and more. We have live actors; we have voice: volume, timbre, pace, etc. We have movement. We have stage pictures. We have scenery, props, costumes, lighting, sound effects, and makeup. We have all these tools at our disposal to tell the story. It's our job to think about the use of all these things. We don't have to create them all, we just need to be in control of their use so that the story is told the way that we want it told.

So I assemble a team of artists and craftsmen: the production team. I realize that in some community theatres that means having a production meeting with your paid staff of designers; but in most community theatres it means begging your friend Bill to "do" scenery, Alice to "do" costumes, etc. Lots of community theatres have volunteer "producers" who assemble a production team and then kind of oversee the team as it functions. However the team is assembled, I now have a bunch of artists who are going to contribute to my telling of the story. We all need to share the same vision. My vision—I need to gather them together and tell them what my vision is and how each of them can contribute their own talents to telling our story. I have made the play available to them to read in advance of the first meeting. When we get together, I begin by discussing what the play is about, in what period it is set, what the style is (realistic, abstract, etc.), what the circumstances are, who the characters are, and their relationships and major motivations. I talk about how I see the tone of the play: light and bright; dark and foreboding; the texture might be burlap or it might be silk. I talk about my needs for staging: levels, doors, staircases, color, special effects, area lighting, costuming. I do not try to get a complete production concept at that first meeting. What I want to do is get my fellow artists excited about the project and then turn them loose to think about what they might do to contribute to the telling of the story. They should take my general comments as a jumping-off place for their own creativity. I encourage them to consider what is possible and what tools they have that will help them make a statement about the play and its meaning.

In subsequent production meetings, each of the members of the team presents his or her ideas. *This is a very important time in the production process.* ***AND IT'S TRICKY!*** The reason it's important is that each member of the team needs to feel important in contributing to the production. Each of them needs to feel *OWNERSHIP.* They need to feel as though their ideas were seriously considered and had an impact on the final concept. If they can feel that way, they will work tirelessly to make the production a success. Now, the reason it's tricky is that I probably can't use every idea that everyone brings to the meeting. I have to be very careful to consider each idea, to judge its merits, and see if it will work to tell the story in the way I have in mind. I cannot imagine saying to a designer, "No, that is totally wrong." I can meet with each of the designers individually, and I will later, but at this stage of design concept planning I find it useful to have everyone there and in on the discussion. I have had a technical director comment, after hearing a scene design presentation, "You know, I was thinking, what if we turned that platform ninety degrees. You'd have the space you need for that bit you want to do in Act Two and the door would be more center." The scenic designer and I looked at each other and I said, "Of course. That solves it." I had a lighting designer who contributed greatly to the finished design of our set for *Amadeus*. I've got all these creative types at my disposal, so I use them. I might not make a final decision on things this early in the process, because I may want to go back to my script and see how the ideas presented to me affect what I want to do. For example, the scenic designer may have taken my suggestion of using levels a little too far and given me a three-step up to a platform. It looks good on paper, but on reflection with script in hand, I can see that there might be a problem getting the speed of a cross to work with that many steps. Maybe two would be better. So we talk and make a decision.

But—*AND THIS IS IMPORTANT*—I can't put off making final decisions too long, or the whole production process comes to a halt. The costume designer needs to know what colors the scenic designer is going to use. The lighting designer needs to know where he can hang lights. He also needs to know what colors the other designers are using. And once these decisions are made, any changes have to be discussed with all involved. I once had a scenic designer who decided (on his own) to substitute a red sofa for the one we had agreed on. Imagine the distress the costume designer felt at dress rehearsal when the leading lady, dressed in a beautiful and expensive red dress, sat on that sofa. We need to talk to each other, people!

CHAPTER TWO

BLOCKING

Telling the Story Through Blocking

I feel that blocking a play is one of the most important things I do. I want to be in control of all the movements the actors make. It is important because actor movement and placement are vital in telling the story. Blocking is what Jon Jory calls the "visual score" of a production. I like that description because it implies that there is a plan. And let me say right here that I'm a strong believer in pre-blocking a show. I plan out, before rehearsals start, every movement that every actor will make. I leave nothing to "figure out later.' That doesn't mean that I might not change something when I find out that what I had created just doesn't work. If something doesn't work in any aspect of the production, I change it. I know there are some directors who do not plan out their blocking; they let the actors "find it" during rehearsal. My opinion is that they are lazy and crazy. Directors are in charge of telling the story; actor movement and placement tell the story. Hello?

OK, so how does blocking help tell the story? Well, first of all, actor placement can show relationships among characters, which are important for the audience to understand. A deaf person should be able to watch the play and still understand what is going on—almost like watching a film in a foreign language. The way people interact says something about their relationship. Two people sitting on a couch *next to each other* says one thing; but put those same people on the couch *at either end*, it says something else.

Take one of those people, have him get up from the couch and move away, leaving his back to the other. It says something about what is happening in their relationship. Suppose in the next bit of dialogue he turns at something she says and he crosses and sits next to her on the couch. What she said persuaded him to return and sit close. It says something about them. But what if what she says causes him to retreat even further upstage to the bar to fix himself a drink, and a couple of lines later he exits upstage, leaving her alone? What do those movements have to say about their relationship and, thereby, the story? One might say, "Well, the author says 'he exits' so he has to exit." Precisely! The author has him exit for a reason, and we can help the audience understand that reason by the way we prepare for that exit.

Here's another example of showing relationship—and then, of course, storytelling—through actor movement and placement: In our play, the main character has angered the town, and a number of the townspeople come to his house to confront him. Let's say they enter by the front door, stage left. They are let in by a housekeeper, who then disappears. Our hero is standing stage right. We can help the audience understand what is happening in this scene by the way we move the actors. If the townspeople move to stage center and our hero steps farther stage right, it would seem that the group is in control of the scene and forcing our hero to retreat. If, slowly, the dialogue indicates that our hero starts to gain some strength in this confrontation, we could move him more center, maybe even face-to-face with them. He appears to be as strong as them. Visually, we have a stalemated confrontation. Something has to happen.

If the group wins, our hero retreats to stage right and the group exits. If our hero wins, the group exits stage left and our hero crosses behind them and closes the door. The way this scene is blocked will help the audience understand the story. Here is another example—one that I like to use in workshops. It works best using a blackboard, so you'll just have to use your imagination. The play is an historical drama about a king and one of his knights. The scenic designer has given me a set of steps that ascend from center stage to stage left. The play opens with the king in control of his subjects, particularly the knight. So we put him at the top of the steps and the knight, kneeling, at the bottom. During the course of the action, the knight asserts himself in his struggle to gain control. He stands and crosses up a few steps. The king, in response to this challenge, loses absolute authority, and in thwarting the action by the knight, crosses down a few steps. The action of the play continues to show the balance of power is slowly shifting to the knight. He moves farther up the steps and the king moves farther down.

When they seem to be of equal strength, they are on the same level. By the end of the play, the knight has assumed the power and the king has lost everything. So their positions are opposite from what they were from the beginning of the play. If we did this play using gibberish for language, the audience would still know what's going on. Which reminds me: when we watch a film in a foreign language, we might not know exactly what the characters are saying, but we know precisely what is going on just by the way in which they physically deal with each other. Put the "mute" on your TV and watch a program. We should be able to put a "mute" on our stage production and still tell the story.

So the first step in blocking, for me, is to break the play into units. Some directors call these units "French scenes" or "motivational units" or, very commonly, "beats." Whatever they are called, they serve the same purpose. The unit starts. As soon as the subject changes or a new idea is introduced, as soon as another character enters that changes the course of the conversation, this is the start of a new unit. Within each unit there are forces at work that carry the action forward. There are conflicts, tactics, obstacles; some in the dialogue and some in the subtext. Each character wants something in each unit.

Dividing the play into these units prevents us from being overwhelmed at the task of analyzing the play and trying to figure out how to make it work. To start on page one and say, "OK, I'm going to block this play," would be a daunting task. However, if one says, "OK, what is happening in this three-or four-page unit? What are the forces at work? I know what the characters are saying, but what are they thinking?"

With those decisions made, it is now possible to block the scene to make it clear to the audience what is happening. An example: Suppose there is a scene in which a young man and woman are sitting on a swing on the porch of her family home and it's a hot summer night. It doesn't make any difference what they are talking about; they can be talking about the weather, the old dog across the street, about him saving his money up so he can buy a car, anything. What they are thinking is altogether different. Both have romance in mind. He's thinking about the same kiss she's thinking about. They both have goals. He must take some action to accomplish his goal. Her action would be to seem receptive to his action, which would accomplish her goal. What obstacle is in the way? Her parents are right inside and could appear at any second. In this example, we have a nice understandable unit. Easy to block. And, we have *SUBTEXT!*— what they are thinking. (More about that later.)

Using this same example, suppose that the young woman's mother appears on the porch. Now we have a whole new set of circumstances. The young people's immediate goal (the kiss) has been put on hold. There are now different forces at work. This is a new unit. The subject of conversation has changed. The tensions are different. The young man may be so uncomfortable under the penetrating look from the mother that he gets up and maybe even offers her his seat. If this is indicated in the script through dialogue ("Take my seat...." "Thanks.") we will do this blocking as indicated. However, if it is not in the dialogue, we might have him stand and gesture to "take my seat," and she could accept or not. Our choice. And we can't be wrong! We can block this to show what we think is going on in this unit.

To continue with the same scene, the young woman decides to go inside the house to get some lemonade. The mother and the young man are left alone. We know what they are saying, but what they are thinking is more important. Without actually writing the play right here, it's safe to say that each of the characters has a goal in this new unit. So we can block this unit using these goals, tensions, and obstacles.

See how easy it is to block once we know what the scene is about? Where does blocking come from? Well, basically, it comes from the imagination. You have to see it in your mind's eye. I find myself visualizing the action from very close range—almost as though I was in the scene. Maybe not that close, but at least standing on the apron of the stage. Many directors see the action from much farther back, say halfway back in the auditorium. For me, that vision comes later when I start to look at stage composition.

One thing I usually avoid is using the blocking notations in the script. There are a number of reasons for this decision. First of all, these notations ("He sits") are not put in the script by the author; they are notes taken by the original stage manager of the original production. This is the blocking of the director who staged it for Broadway. Why would I want to copy his production? I want to do my own production of this play.

Second, the stage manager's notations often are not accurate. I can't tell you the number of times I've read, "He sits" and two pages later it says, "He sits." When did he get up? The stage manager was distracted by calling a light cue on the intervening page and didn't write down, "He stands."

Another reason is that our set may not be exactly the same as that used in the Broadway production. The limitations of the tools with which we have to work—i.e., space, scenery, lighting, etc. are going to call for some changes. And maybe, just maybe, we have a better way to stage this play.

Now there are some things that authors do write in their plays that they feel are the right action for the moment. "She grabs the book" or "He raises his glass to toast" or "She rushes madly to the window" or "They kiss." I would probably use those. How do I tell the difference between what the author has written and what the stage manager has noted? Usually, the author's words are more descriptive. Using the example above, I'm sure the author would write, "She rushes madly to the window." A stage manager's notes would read, "Crosses to window," or "Cross right." Authors write, "He slumps into the chair." Stage managers notes, "Sits."

Do you remember all those notes I took when I first started reading the play? Those in the left-hand margin? Now is a good time to look at those. In my first read-through, I saw, in a unit, two actors on each side of a table facing each other. That was my immediate visualization of what was happening in that unit. Now I am about to block that unit. So I need to see if my original visualization still is valid. If it is, I use it. If not, I discard it and erase it from the margin.

Now is when I look specifically at those ten or twelve storytelling moments that create the arc of the play. I might first block those units that contain these moments. I need to know where everyone is so the audience "gets it." Since this is a stage picture I am getting ready to "snap," I must plan ahead so that the characters' movements leading up to this moment are logical and motivated. If a character's reaction to a surprise entrance of another character coming down the staircase is important for the audience to see, he has to be in a position to take focus. In the dialogue leading up to that moment, I must find a logical reason for that character to move to that position. So, starting at the beginning of that unit, I can see where he is and I know where he has to be. I find some reason—relationship, tension, or business—to get him where he needs to be. Sometimes I may have to resort to a purely mechanical reason for a cross to the proper position. But it has to be made to appear logical. Let's say I need this character up right. He is stage left. He has a glass in his hand. He downs his drink and crosses to stage right to put his glass on the bar. As he listens and responds to the next couple lines of dialogue, he crosses to just downstage of the staircase, which is where he has to be for the moment when the surprise entrance happens. If I had left him stage left for this entrance, his reaction to the entrance would be missed because he was out of the focal point. His reaction is what is important.

It is a storytelling moment. It needs to be seen. So I put him at the focal point (that point where I want the audience's attention).

As I study the script with blocking in mind, I feel impulses for characters to move. There are lines that just scream, "Get up, cross away," or "He turns and takes a step toward her"—stuff like that. I rely on those impulses. I write them down as blocking, and if they don't work I get rid of them. During blocking rehearsals, which I will discuss a little later, I often have actors who have different impulses for a given moment. An actor will say, "Can I move on this line?" He's interpreting also; he is a fellow artist and if he feels like his character just needs to show what he is thinking at that moment, his impulse to move may be better than mine. So we try it. If it doesn't completely destroy something I have prepared, I go with his creation. After all, just because I thought of it doesn't make it wonderful.

One of the things that I try to avoid at all costs is unmotivated movement. You know, like, "those two characters have been in the same positions for the last few lines, so maybe I better have him cross to the left of her and then to keep it interesting I'll have him move back to her and then cross to her right." What do those crosses have to do with anything? What is important to keep in mind is that a director should not confuse activity with action. Action deals with what is happening in the scene—the dynamics, the tension, the conflicts. Activity deals with what they are doing, not what they are thinking.

The scene with the young boy and girl on the porch might have the activity of the boy playing with a yo-yo and the girl addressing invitations to a party. But that's not what they are thinking about. The scene is not about the yo-yo or the invitations. It's about what is happening between them. There are movements that are appropriate for an activity the characters are involved in: "She crosses to the coffee table to pour herself some tea," or, in the above example of the man going to the bar for a drink, "He moves left of her as he crosses to the bar to refresh his drink." But, you see, he might also make that same move to her left and to the bar to show that he needs to separate himself from her. That is action. Just to move left of her says nothing. Unmotivated activity. Remember what I said about blocking being the "visual score?" Every movement needs to tell the story.

I have adjudicated play festivals all over the country and, without fail, somewhere in the festival I will see this blocking: Two people are sitting on a couch center and a third person is sitting in a chair stage right center. They have been sitting there for several minutes. What they are talking about is engrossing and important to the story, but the director feels they have been sitting there too long, so he has the person stage right rise and cross upstage of the couch. To make matters worse, the director has one of the seated characters stand and cross and sit in the chair that was just vacated. For no apparent reason! First of all, the director failed to see that the action of the play was moving forward with the dialogue and didn't trust that it held the audience's attention and so decided to add some activity to make it visually more interesting.

I once saw a production of *Three Viewings* in which the one woman in the scene sat in a chair for thirty minutes and spoke to us. I was riveted! If the director hadn't trusted the material and had given her an activity, the impact would have been completely lost.

We are, after all, trying to give the illusion of real life. If you are having a conversation with some people in your living room and someone gets out of their chair to go warm themselves by the fire, you do not get out of your chair and go sit in the one that was just vacated. We don't do that. Once someone sits in a chair, it's theirs. You can't sit there unless you ask and receive permission. If you went out to the kitchen for some more ice and came back to find someone sitting in your chair, you would be annoyed.

Another thing to consider in blocking is the environment in which the characters are living. What the setting provides for is what we call *business*. In real life we seldom just stand and talk to each other. Normally we are engaged in another activity. At the early stages of planning the production, we have not yet seen the set fully decorated by the designer. So we must imagine what is in this space. The decoration should say something about the people who live there. If it is a living room, what's in the room? Are these people readers? Is there a bookcase? A coffee table with magazines? Are there windows with drapes that need to be opened or closed? Is there a desk where one might sit and write or read an important letter? What do the characters bring onstage with them? A purse? Some knitting? The evening paper? A briefcase? A tray of drinks? Or let's suppose it's a scene in a kitchen. We know how everyone congregates in a kitchen. What is everyone doing? Is someone cooking or setting the breakfast table? Cleaning up after a meal? Putting groceries away? If so who would help and who would not? What are all the activities that take place in a kitchen?

There are sinks and refrigerators and cupboards and stoves and silverware and knives and food. The characters may be discussing something very important in their lives and in the action of the play, but they are doing something else. This is business. If we don't include business in our planning of the scene, the action of the play will seem sterile and unrealistic. So, imagine what's in the space and use it.

Let me give you an example from my own experience. I was doing a production of *To Kill a Mockingbird* on a very wide stage—so wide, in fact, that most of the stage was empty. Atticus' house was way over stage right. So any scenes that happened in the middle of the stage would be people standing on the same level with little or nothing to provide any kind of business except for character business. I felt I needed to give this area something that would provide for some interesting stage pictures and movement. I hit upon the idea of an old well and sold the idea to the designer. The result was that the kids played on it, hid behind it, jumped off it, lay on it, sat and talked on it. Other characters sat on it or stood on either side of it facing each other (showing a relationship). And the scene where Atticus and Scout talk and the stage directions suggest that it takes place on Atticus' porch, I moved it to the well, where it could be seen and heard by everyone and, in isolated light, made a wonderful stage picture.

Here is something else to watch for. Important speeches should probably be played back onto the stage, rather than towards offstage. I gave you an example earlier in staging the porch scene in *Over the River and Through the Woods*. Let me remind you of the point I was making: If characters John and Bill are playing a scene together and they are at extreme stage right and John has most of the dialogue and the most important speech, he should probably be right of Bill, bringing the scene back onto the stage. If not, audience members in house right (actors' left) will be looking at John in profile and Bill straight on, giving Bill the focus. John should have the focus (unless Bill's reaction to John is more important than what John is saying). So, in planning blocking, I find a way to get John right of Bill. In planning my blocking, I try to make the length of the cross fit the length of the line. It can be awkward for an actor to have to cross— say, from up right to down left—on a three or four word-speech. If I need the actor to be down left, then I had better break that cross into to two sections or find a way to have him closer to down left to make that cross.

Not every move by an actor should start on the very first word of his speech. The impulse to move may be later in the speech. I look for those impulses. Often movement can be used as punctuation. A character may sit to close an idea or stand to start a new subject. Imagine, in a heated argument, a character makes his final point; and he sits to close his argument. Or he is sitting and he stands and says, "But, have you considered this?"

I try to avoid having actors standing in a straight line. It is unnatural and not a very interesting stage picture. Usually it happens by accident, or the actors are not quite where they are supposed to be. If this happens, I find some way to break the line up; I change the blocking by moving actors around. I try to find interesting body positions for the actors to play a scene. Many times, if everyone is standing, say, in a living room scene, it doesn't seem natural. (As far as I'm concerned, the only time people stand around and talk is at a cocktail party.) Two characters sitting next to each other on a sofa might be made more interesting to look at if one sits on the arm of the sofa, or one sits facing front and the other is in profile.

Blocking Notations

The next step for me is to make the blocking notations in my script. First of all, I like to make these notations in the outside margin of the page. That way, the blocking can be read easily during blocking rehearsals. When I'm blocking actors into a scene, I do not have to wade through a whole lot of interp stuff to see where an actor is supposed to move. All the interp notes are on the inside margin. Later, long after blocking rehearsals are over, I add the technical notes in the outside margin—things like, "Lights change," or "Drop comes in."

Now this is my method. Every director has his or her own and they all work. Let's say the first blocking on a page is for Sam to stand and cross right. At the exact point in the dialogue where I want this to happen, I put the number"1" and draw a small circle around it. In the outside margin I put an identical "1" with a circle around it. Next to that number, I make a shorthand notation about what the character is supposed to do. In this case, I would write "S" for Sam...then an arrow "^" pointing up to indicate that he is supposed to stand... and then "X," meaning for him to cross; and finally an "R" to indicate the direction of the move. So my notation would look like this: "S^XR." This blocking would indicate that I had intended for the actor to move all the way to the right side of the stage. That could be a big area. If there is a window stage right and I want the actor to cross to the window, I might indicate that in my notation by adding the shorthand for "to," which is "2," and "window," which is "win." So then my notation would look like this: "S^XR2win."

The next move by a character is "2" in a circle and written in the exact place this movement is supposed to happen. It is then noted in the outside margin, as before. When the entire page has been blocked, there should be a number of circles with numbers written in the text and corresponding circles with numbers and blocking notations in the outside column. When I turn the page and continue blocking, I always start over with "1" in a circle for the first move on that page. The numbers are not important beyond a reference for the notations.

In some complicated blocking or grouping of characters, I often draw a picture to show the relationships of the characters. This picture is an overhead view, using a circle to indicate a person's head; inside the circle is the character's initial, and attached to the circle is a small "v" representing the character's nose to indicate which way he is facing. I find this particularly helpful if there are a number of characters onstage. Many times I have had to draw such a picture at the bottom of the page to show where everyone is at that moment. When I turn the page to continue blocking, I can use it as a quick reference to see where I left a character.

Everyone has their own shorthand for blocking notes. Each just makes up whatever works for them. The point is to keep it as simple as possible so that it isn't taking up the whole margin. For a more definitive discussion of blocking notations, I recommend you read *The Art and Craft of Stage Management*, published by Samuel French. There is a chapter entitled, "Traditionally Used Symbols, Abbreviations, and Terms." It is so extensive you may not be able to use all of it, but there is a lot you can use. So now I have the entire play blocked on paper and can begin the actual staging of what was in my head.

Now I have to find the actors.

CHAPTER THREE

AUDITONING ACTORS

Director Preparation

First of all, I draw a chart that shows in the left-hand column the name of each character, one under the other. Across the top of the page, I note the page numbers of the "beats" or "motivational units." For instance, pages 4 through 8 might be a convenient unit to use in auditions and in rehearsals. In the column below the page numbers, I place an "X" in the row opposite the character's name, to indicate that the character is in that unit. When I can determine that there are, say, three or four characters in a particular unit, I can decide if it is a good unit to use at auditions. Often the units I use are those "storytelling moments." If it gives the actors a chance to play a nice scene, I make a note of it. If there is a character that requires an unusual quality—a giddy young schoolgirl—I need to find a good unit for a young actress to show me she can break through her natural shyness and give me that quality. Some units are not good for auditions. I need to see if the actors can play a quality I'm looking for. If the unit has this opportunity, I use it. If a unit has a lot of action—running, fighting, etc—it may not work for auditions. If there is a unit that requires a long, loving kiss, I won't use it for the simple reason that the two people could be terribly embarrassed. If the unit has too many characters in it, it will be difficult to use during auditions because my focus will be split too many ways. I only want to hear three or four actors at a time. Two is ideal. Incidentally, I use this same chart method when I start to prepare the rehearsal schedule. In fact, I may use the same chart. (See the section on rehearsal scheduling.)

AUDITIONING ACTORS

Going into auditions, I want to know as much about the characters as possible. If there are references in the dialogue to their height, weight, look, or ethnicity, I need to be looking for those types of people as I hear them read. We don't usually get exactly what we need at auditions, so during the audition process, I try to see what possibilities exist with who shows up. After all, in community theatre we have to cast from those who choose to audition. I realize there is the "beating the bushes" to find the right people for the show, but every effort should be made to cast those that have a desire to be in the production. They made the effort to come to the audition, so they should be given preferential treatment. Besides, if you have to beg a person to be in the show, he or she may feel they are doing you a favor and, consequently, may give you problems later on. I recently had auditions for a production that required seventeen men. At auditions, not one man showed up. Talk about "beat the bushes."

All was fine except for one actor who held me for ransom over his rehearsal schedule. But, let's face it, casting in community theatre means you're going to make do with what you have. In the professional theatre the director would merely say, "Next," and look at a number of actors until he got exactly what he wanted. Ah, the luxury. But for us, "Ah, the challenge." I once worked with a director who insisted that all the Pacific Islanders in *Teahouse of the August Moon* had to have dark brown eyes. No blue-eyed people need apply. That was a tough casting process. This same director, who himself was very short, was conscious of everyone's height. He would not cast people of varying heights unless the script called for a very tall person—whereupon he would cast only short people and the appropriate "tall" person, even though that person might be of only medium height. Well, I must confess, it worked, but what stress the director put upon himself. One last word about preparation for the audition. It is helpful to have an audition card or

41

form. The actor should fill it out upon arrival. It should have a space for all the important stuff you want to know: name, address, phone number, male/female, age (or birth date), roles they have done before and at which theater and when, classes or training, will they shave beards and mustaches, will they dye hair, roles they would like to be considered for or will accept only, and—crucial to the director's sanity— *CONFLICTS*. (If someone works three nights a week, it will be difficult to plan a rehearsal schedule.) (My personal favorite is the actor who wrote he could be there every night but opening night.) There also should be a line where they can indicate if they will work on the show if they are not cast.

Some theatres where I have worked will take a snapshot of each person and attach it to the audition card. This is extremely helpful.

Preparing the actors for the audition

I think it is important that everyone should feel welcome and relaxed and as comfortable as possible. These are scary times, especially for first-time people. I try to make my personal demeanor as nonjudgmental as possible. I tell everyone, "Hey, this whole thing is not a judgment on you as a person; if you are not cast, it doesn't mean you are a bad person or unworthy. It only means, in my judgment, for this show, you might not be right because of the way I see the role being played." Sometimes I relate a story about Dustin Hoffman. At a conference I observed, he answered a question from one of the students about how he handled nervousness at auditions. He told them that he was into boxing. Not as a boxer, but that he liked boxing. A boxer goes down to the gym, he told them, and works out, sparring against another boxer for a few rounds, takes a shower, and goes home. He has done his "craft" for a little while. He told the students he took the pressure off himself at auditions by thinking of the audition as a chance to act, or "practice his craft," for a few minutes. He told them that there were twelve other guys in the room who were probably going to get the role, but at least he got to act for a few minutes.

In addition to all this, I talk about what the play is about in general terms. Often, in community theatre, people auditioning have not read the play ahead of time. They have no idea about who the characters are. So I give general descriptions of their personalities and their situations—enough information so that when I call upon them to read for a certain character, they have a starting point. They probably won't remember, so I will have to repeat it later.

So, what do I look for at auditions? I have been asked that question many times. The interesting thing is that I usually tell those auditioning exactly what I am looking for Included in my "welcome speech" are a number of things that I will be looking for as they audition. I tell them: "First off, I want to know whether you can read. I want to know whether or not you can read the dialogue and make it sound like real speech. Second, I want to see a spark of creativity, that is, can you make something out of what you are reading? Do you show any indication of understanding what you're talking about? I want to see some of your own personality. Do you show good instincts? If I cast you, what am I going to be working with? Can I get a performance out of you?"

The physical attributes of the actor are secondary, in my opinion. The audience normally has no preconceived notions of what a character should look like. When the curtain goes up, they will accept exactly whatever you give them. Tall or short, lean or fat, old or young, they will believe, because they want to believe. (I recently saw a production of *Driving Miss Daisy* where the man playing Hoke was twenty-three years old, not age appropriate at all. But through his fine work, the audience quickly accepted him as being much older than he actually was.) The point is, I think more about what the actor is going to give me rather than what he looks like. It makes the job a lot easier. I do believe, however, that if at all possible, the roles should be cast age appropriate. It is often very difficult for audiences to believe that a twenty-year-old is the mother of a fifty year-old.

Years ago, I had a university theatre professor work for me as a guest director. He was used to casting young people in roles they were too young for. After auditions he showed me his possible cast list. He did, indeed, have a twenty-year-old cast as the grandmother in *The Royal Family*. The girl was a good actress, but about sixty years too young. There was no way our audiences would accept that. I did not approve his casting and he went back to the drawing board.

When I invite a person I have never seen before to read for me, I look closely at the information sheet they have filled out. Hopefully, there will be something on that sheet that I can comment on that will help put them at ease and give them a sense of contact with me. You know, something like, "Oh, I see you live in Portage. Where do you live? I also live in Portage." Or, "I see you played Nurse Ratchet, at East Lyons Community Theatre. What a great role! That must have been wonderful to play her." Something. Anything that occurs to me. I just say it, even if I don't know where it's going.

There are a lot of "rookies" at community theatre auditions. They have no idea how this all works. So I tell them: first we're going to do this and then we're going to do that. I explain the whole process. Normally, but not always, a "rookie" will not give you a good reading if you call on them first to read. They don't know what they are doing, what is expected, or how to do it. I try to get someone to read first who has some experience, to kind of "set the pace." I try to use someone who I know can read and is a possible candidate for a role. (Don't forget: people will surprise you.) A "rookie" will hear the reading and say, "OK, I get it." and when asked to read they will come before you with some understanding of what is expected.

A new person, who has never auditioned before, is rather unlikely to give me much. She may be able to read the words and not much else. They may need some direction or, at least, some encouragement. I try to do that in a way that is not threatening. To avoid embarrassing a person, I like to go up to them after they have read and give them suggestions about what is needed in their reading. Then I have them read the same scene again. I can find out if they can take direction.

I think community theatre auditions must be as fair as possible. One of the ways I try to achieve this is to make sure that everyone, no matter how badly they read or how "uncastable" they are, gets a chance to read at least twice. So someone reads for me that is way too young or too old. So what? If they get a chance to read a couple of times, they have had a fair hearing and cannot complain that they didn't have a chance. Who knows? That person may end up volunteering to work on the crew if they thought they were fairly treated. The most popular notion about community theatre auditions is that the director has precast all the roles. It is a common complaint: "Well, I'm not going to audition because I know who is going to get the role." Hello! They got it because you didn't audition. We see a lot of the same people on our local stages because they are the ones who audition.

The Audition

If I have a large crowd at auditions, it may not be possible to give everyone a chance to read twice that night. So I always invite the unlucky ones to come back the second night (For *Steel Magnolias* we had 120 women audition. It took a week). As I read through all the people, I usually can get an idea of who may be able to play certain roles. When I start reading people in combinations, I try to slip in a combination of those people I think are strong candidates to play the lead roles. Before I make my decisions, I like to see if what I am thinking is possible. Since I normally read people in several combinations, I'm usually successful in disguising what I'm doing. If I can't do it without being obvious, I don't do it. Maybe at callbacks, but not at initial auditions.

Now let me say a few words about taking notes during auditions. There is no right or wrong way. What I do is, on a yellow legal pad, write down the name of the actor and the name of the role they are reading. Once I have written down all that information, I give them some clues as to what the unit is about and maybe some character information, if I haven't already done that during my introductory speech. As the actors begin reading, I make some short, cryptic notes about their readings. For instance, I might write things such as: "Can read; Good instincts; Moves well; Good personality; Can use; Could play Harry; Not right for Harry, read for Paul." Or my notes might say, "Does not read well; Little comprehension, Too young for Sally, read for Sarah; Can not use; Would be a challenge." The point is, I need to have some written reaction to an actor's reading, but I don't want to spend the whole time writing. I need to see and hear them. On my notepad, in the left-hand margin, if an actor is a possible for a certain role, I write the name of the character. That way, when I reread that actor, I have a specific reason for reading him/her, not just giving them a second chance.

I try to organize the audition cards on the table in front of me into four or five piles: Younger men, Older men, Younger women, Older women, and Children. That way, I don't have to sort through all the cards when I call up people to read. The audition cards I organize so that I call up the actor who is on the top of the pile and after I have read him/her, that card goes on the bottom so that he doesn't read again until all others in that category have read.

After I have read everyone twice, I ask all the actors who are present, if there is any role they would like to read for that they didn't have a chance to read. Some of the responses may lead me to think, *What are you thinking. Get real.* On the other hand, my thoughts might be, *Interesting! I never thought of that.* It may be a waste of time, but it also may be valuable. It certainly helps with the "fairness" issue.

Callbacks.

Hopefully, callbacks are necessary. I like to prepare for callbacks by making a plan for who is going to read what. Here is the way I do it. On a yellow legal pad I note each unit I want to read, say pages 45 through 49. I list each character in that unit across the row and under each character I place the names of the actors who are possible candidates for that role.

So it might look something like this:

Pages 45-49

Characters:	Willy	Linda	Biff
Actors:	Brown	Green	Smith
	Centers	Johnson	Gordon
	Helms	Gover	Mason
	Helms	Green	Gordon
	Brown	Johnson	Mason

I do this organization beforehand so that I don't waste people's time during the audition having them to wait for me to figure out who is going to read with whom. And, of course, I want to see how certain combinations work. In community theatre, I have found that sometimes there is someone who will call and ask if they can still audition (she wasn't able to make the original auditions because they were out of town).

When this happens, I try to accommodate that person. However, if I end up casting that person, I run the risk of the old complaint, "Oh, he was precast. He didn't even go to auditions." So I have to be careful about that. Everyone who had auditioned needs to know that I was being accommodating.

Now I've auditioned all the actors, and I have all my notes. It's decision time. Who gets cast in which role is my decision alone. However, I find it helpful to discuss the possibilities with my stage manager and my assistant director (if I have one.) Together we list all the roles and all the possible people to play them. Usually I take the lead and say who I like for each role and why. Often it is obvious that a particular actor is perfect for a certain role—he reads well, understands the character, and is physically right. He may not be exactly what I had in mind at the start of the audition process, but he comes closer than anyone else. Then there is the actor who gave a good audition, but is not what I had in mind for the role for which she is best suited. This is where instinct takes over. I consult my notes to determine if the actor can take direction, and if I believe I can make this work. Assuming I have a choice, I go with my instincts. (I once cast a huge man to play a little old grandfather. He read well, but I thought, *Wrong!* It turned out, he was fabulous.) More times than not, I have had to cast an unskilled actor, knowing that he will be a "challenge." I find myself thinking, *Can I get a performance out of this person?* I always try to fill the roles with the good actors, but this is community theatre, and we have to make concessions. If we don't, we won't have a cast.

There are other factors in the decision process—things like: Do they look like they could be married? Do they look like a family? Will we give away who the villain is, because the actor looks villainous? Is the actor physically able to run up and down the stairs as required? From what we know about this actor, is she capable of learning the lines? Has this actor had all the lead roles in the past year? Does this actor have a history of being late, being difficult to work with, or being disruptive? Can I reasonably work around this actor's conflicts? These types of things, and many, many more affect decisions.

Those assisting me in the decision-making, are free to say who they like for the roles and why. I listen to their reasons and take them under advisement. After everyone has had their say, I gather up all the notes and the audition cards. I take them home to study and to "sleep on it." In one or two days I will come to a decision based on reality and instinct.

At the theatre where I worked for thirty-eight years, the tradition was to post the cast list on the window of the stage door for all to come and see—noon on Friday. I made a decision not to be anywhere near that door at noon on Friday. That decision was made one day when I was not thinking and I was headed out that door to go to lunch. There, outside the door, reading the posted cast list, was a group of people. Their reactions to not being cast were too painful to watch. So, I decided to post the cast list and leave for lunch out another door.

Actually, I think another way of announcing the cast is better. I think either the director or the stage manager should call all who auditioned and inform them of the decisions. Those who were cast need to know about picking up scripts and attending the first rehearsal. Those who were not cast need to be encouraged to work on the crew, or at least to come back to the next audition. If I make those calls, I often get questions from those not cast wanting to know why they weren't cast, or, maybe, how they can get better. This is often productive. But sometimes it is hard to do.

Some theatres announce the casting results by e-mail. Some post it on their Web sites. Both work well, I think. But I still like the personal touch.

For me, the hardest thing is not to cast a close friend. It hurts, because I know how much they want the role. But I have to do what I think is best for the show. That's my job. I once did not cast a friend in a show, and she was so angry she would not speak to me. I ended up writing her a letter in which I told her that I was disappointed in her reaction because I didn't realize that our friendship was based on whether I cast her or not. She appeared at the theatre the next day to apologize.

CHAPTER FOUR

REHEARSALS

I love rehearsing. I look forward to every rehearsal. Sometimes I can hardly wait for a rehearsal to begin. "What are we going to create tonight?" OK, OK. Blocking rehearsals are not that thrilling. But if I look at blocking as seeing what was in my head is now being done with actors, it can be somewhat stimulating. I, personally, am very process oriented. That is, I love getting the show ready: working with actors and technicians and designers.

We are all creating a piece of art and I hold the brush. (That was a bit corny, wasn't it? Sorry). The point is, it's an exciting time, especially if you have good and talented people to work with.

The Rehearsal Schedule.

On a calendar I put everyone's conflicts. (There are always conflicts; this is community theatre, after all.) When I can see these conflicts laid out before me on a calendar, I can start to plan which actors I need (and can get) on which nights. I like to plan a rehearsal schedule backwards starting with the final dress rehearsal back to the first rehearsal. If there are going to be twenty-five rehearsals, I want to plan what is going to happen at each one of them. I normally take a calendar and count backwards from opening night. Every theatre operates differently, but a happy situation for me would be one where "final dress" is the night before opening night. "Of course," you might say.

But I know a theatre that does not rehearse the night before they open. Anyway, to continue with the "happy situation," let's say opening night is on a Friday. Thursday then becomes final dress. Some theatres have an invited audience for that rehearsal. I'm somewhat opposed to that for the following reason: Invited dress rehearsal audiences are often made up of friends of the cast and crew. They are going to be a great audience, especially for a comedy. They will laugh their heads off at everything. The actors will be exhilarated. Now, what do they have to look forward to on opening night? And when the general audience doesn't laugh like their friends did the night before, there can be a letdown and some disappointment. You've heard of the "second-night letdown." Why would you want it on your opening night? I realize this decision for an invited audience isn't always in my control (each theatre has its traditions), but given a choice, I would prefer to have the invited audience for Wednesday's dress rehearsal.

Still working backwards, Tuesday before opening, the lighting and scenery should finally be ready for looking at makeup and costumes in the stage light. (Remember, I said this was a "happy situation.) Monday's rehearsal I call "dress and tech." It sometimes is the first time the actors appear in costumes. (Some costumers don't want their creations destroyed in a technical rehearsal.) It's also when I found out that the set designer had forgotten that the costumer had built this beautiful and expensive red dress for the lead actress and had brought in a red sofa for her to sit on. The "tech" part of "tech and dress" is usually the first time the tech crew gets to run the show after they have learned their jobs at Sunday's technical rehearsal. If I have the luxury of having the crew and "staff" on the Saturday before Sunday tech, I like to do a "dry tech" (cues without actors). However, for many community theatres, that can be "load-in day," when the scenery is transported from the shop to the stage and is erected.

The final week before I go into tech week, I like to call "run-through week." I work large chunks of the play: whole acts to begin with, saving Thursday and Friday for final run

-throughs of the entire play. No stopping. Curtain up to curtain down. (Imaginary curtain if I'm in a rehearsal room and not on the stage.)

As a general rule, working backwards from there, I schedule larger chunks to rehearse as we get closer to the "run-through" week. We might be doing whole Acts later in the week and just scenes earlier in the week. The next two weeks back I call the "work weeks."

These rehearsals are when we "work" on specific scenes, sections, and beats. Finally, the last week back (the first week of rehearsals) is "blocking and review blocking" week. Normally, I like to begin blocking at the second rehearsal. Some directors, if they have the luxury of time, like to spend a few rehearsals doing "table talk," where the company reads and discusses the play. I have never had that luxury, but it sounds wonderful.

So, how many rehearsals is that from first rehearsal to opening? Assuming five rehearsals a week, which is normal, the number of rehearsals I've scheduled is twenty-five. I have found that sufficient for doing a non-musical. For a musical, because of all the singing and dancing needing to be rehearsed, I like to plan on another four, to make it twenty-nine rehearsals. It really depends on the difficulty of the production and the quality of the performers. One could probably do *Tuesdays with Morrie* in eighteen to twenty, whereas *Jesus Christ Superstar* might not be ready with thirty-five.

Preparing The Rehearsal Schedule.

There are three principles involved in setting up a rehearsal schedule. First, I need to see what I have to accomplish at each rehearsal (Block Scene One). Second, I have to take into account any conflicts the cast may have that would prevent them from attending a rehearsal. (John works on Wednesday evenings until 8 p.m.). Third, I need to use the actors' time as efficiently as possible. (On Thursday, John is not needed until the end of Scene 3, so he does not have to come in before 9 p.m.). There is nothing more aggravating than to show up for rehearsal at 7 p.m. and do nothing until your scene at 9:30. Sometimes it can't be avoided that an actor is in Scene 1 at 7:00 and has to sit around until Scene 5 at 9:30. That's the way it is. But all else being equal (and possible), perhaps those two scenes could be scheduled on separate nights—as a courtesy to the actor.

I normally prepare a rehearsal schedule for a week at a time. I know in the first week I need to block the show and review the blocking. I know the way I work. I should not plan on doing more than twenty pages of blocking a night. So, if the script is sixty pages long, it's going to take me three nights to block and possibly two nights to review: Act I on one night and Act II the next. That's five rehearsals for blocking. Counting the first read-through, there may be six rehearsals in that first week. If that is not possible, Act II will have to be reviewed at the beginning of the next week. Since there is a chance we may not be able to accomplish all the blocking we intended to do, I need to keep next week's schedule flexible. Thus, one week at a time.

Actually, there is one more operative principle in writing a schedule. In trying to accommodate actors' conflicts and using their time efficiently, I need to make sure that each scene or section receives the same amount of rehearsal time. In line with this, a section rehearsed on Sunday should probably be rehearsed again before the next Sunday. If not, much of what was accomplished could be lost.

Let me share with you something I do that is particularly helpful in preparing a rehearsal schedule. On a piece of paper, in the left margin, I make a column of all the characters. Across the top, I put the scenes or sections (maybe using page numbers). Now I put an "X" under each scene or section opposite the character's name to show that they are in a scene. If they only have one line in that scene, I write "1

Line." If I use a lined yellow pad, sideways, the vertical columns are already there. All I have to do is to draw a horizontal line under each character's name.

So this is what it looks like:

ACT I

	Scene 1	Scene 2	Scene 3 (p 18-26)	Scene 3 (p 26-38)	Scene 4	etc.
JOHN	X	X		X	X	
ALICE		X	X	X		
BILL			X	X	X	
POLICEMAN			1 line			

With a large cast, this method works well for me to tell at a glance who is needed to rehearse each scene or section.

The First Rehearsal.

One thing to keep in mind is that everyone involved in the production is volunteering because they seek some sort of enjoyment in creating theatre. Everyone's motivation for getting involved is different: some want to "create art", some want to just meet people and have a social life; some just need a night out; some need to be noticed. Whatever their reason, each person becomes involved for the fun of it. Besides directing the play, the director is in charge of the "fun factor."

Remember my motto for community theatre: *"If it ain't fun, it ain't worth it. But the fun comes from doing good work."*

Almost without exception, the first rehearsal is a combination of dealing with administrative issues, a presentation of the artistic vision for the production, and a read-through of the entire play.

Administrative Issues.

The entire cast and possibly some crew have assembled. Everyone needs to know the rules. In some theatres, a "staff" person will come in and talk about the rules of the theatre—you know, no smoking in the building, clean up after rehearsals, stuff like that. Biography questionnaires for program information may be handed out at this time as well as contact sheets and cast lists; anything that has to do with working on this production. (You may wonder why I put the word "staff" in quotes. A majority of community theatres do not have a professional staff. However, they may have a volunteer who acts as a producer of the production. It could be a member of the board of directors or just an experienced volunteer whose job it is to see that the production elements come together. In that case, that person is acting as "staff.")

Next, I tell the cast what I expect of them—things like being on time for rehearsal. I also tell them that I would like to have them show up for rehearsal ten to fifteen minutes early so that we can start rehearsal exactly on time. They need to come in, do their greetings, hear announcements, settle down, and prepare their minds for what we are about to do.

Some directors like to do extensive warm-ups. I'm not against that, but I have never been a big believer in their value. Some would argue with me. That's fine; it just isn't my thing. I also tell actors that they must be prepared to do most of the work ahead away from rehearsals. They must study—not just learn lines. I expect them to come in each evening having prepared themselves for what is about to be rehearsed. I realize most community theatre actors have day jobs, but they need to be encouraged to find some time in the day to do some study.

In this administrative discussion period, I also discuss, in general terms, what their job is and what my job is. I have a whole section coming up later about directing inexperienced actors, so I won't get into that now.

Sharing the Artistic Vision.

I talk about what kind of play it is, its style, its period, its general theme, and any special things the cast should know, like the background for the play, the author's history, and his works. As an example of the latter, it can be helpful to know that most, if not all, of Neil Simon's plays are based on his actual experiences. *Brighton Beach Memoirs* and *Lost In Yonkers* are about his childhood; *Biloxi Blues,* his army experience and *Chapter Two*, his divorce. If I'm doing one of his plays, I should know where it fits and where it came from. There are lots of books on Neil Simon as well as an autobiography that can give that information. Whatever I find out, I should share with the cast. It makes for a more complete experience.

In the discussion of artistic vision, the cast should see any of the scene and costume designs that are ready. It is helpful for them to envision the setting and what they may be wearing. If the designers are available to present their ideas and sketches, it really helps build a production "company."

The First Read-Through.

Sitting around a table, usually, we read through the play with myself or the stage manager describing any significant action or sound effects. As the actors read, I will often stop them to draw their attention to certain aspects of lines or actions. A line that is especially thematic or plot-important is pointed out. I'm not directing actors at this point, I'm merely bringing their attention to things they should know.

Often community theatre actors do not get the opportunity to read the entire script before this first rehearsal. They have probably read bits and pieces of it during auditions, but might not have read the whole play.

Blocking Rehearsals.

In preparation for the blocking rehearsals, someone—the stage manager, "staff" person or myself—needs to tape the floor plan of the set on the rehearsal room floor. When the cast has gathered for their first blocking rehearsal, I walk around the "set", showing them where the doors are, the windows, the steps, and any other architectural features they'll have to deal with. I also need to point out that the three folding chairs lined up represent a sofa and the card table is really a desk—things like that.

Often there will be people in the cast who have never been onstage before (I once had an actor ask, "What's blocking?"). Therefore, I find it necessary to point out all the positions onstage: center stage, stage right, upstage, downstage, etc. To help them remember "up" from "down," I tell them how and why stages used to slant downward towards the audience. (The "why" comes from the use of single-point-perspective scenery at a time in theatrical history.) Thus we use the terms "above" and "below" when we refer to making a move upstage or downstage of a piece of furniture, or standing in relationship to another actor.

The new actor also needs to be shown how to write his or her blocking in the script. So I do a short lesson: "for that down right cross to John, put a small notation of XDR2J where that movement occurs in the line." I don't go through the entire notation system—it would be too confusing. But, knowing that an arrow pointing down or up means "sit" or "stand" can be helpful in simplifying notations. Experienced actors probably already have their own notation system, so it may not be necessary to include them in this lesson.

The next thing I do is to tell the entire cast that I like to block very specifically. In my pre-blocking preparation, discussed earlier, I know exactly where every character is to be at any one time. When I give the actors their movements, I want them precisely where I had envisioned them. For example, I might say "cross to the down right corner of the sofa." (As I said earlier, most actors feel more secure knowing exactly where they are supposed to be.) Now, I also tell them that when we finish blocking and start to play the scenes, that "down right corner of the sofa" may mean that that is just their acting area and they needn't feel as though they are unable to move about. I realize that sometimes they must be in the exact spot for reasons of focus or an important piece of action, but generally they may move about in order for them to express their character's thoughts and feelings. If a character has a long monologue and the actor is experienced, I may give them a whole area of the stage— down right, for example—to do the speech and let them move about as they feel they want to. An inexperienced actor may need my help in deciding how to move during that speech.

None of my blocking is "written in stone" or even in pen. As we start working the play, I usually find that some of my wonderful ideas aren't so wonderful after all. Some things just don't work the way they did in my head. I have to be flexible and willing to change if what I have created isn't working. And, too, my actors may have some great ideas about how to do something in a way that I hadn't thought of. This is a group process, after all, and I love it when an actor solves a problem for me.

As we block, it is often necessary for me to remind the actors to write their notations in their books. I keep my eye out for that—it prevents actor confusion when we go to review the blocking later. I also try to make sure that they are making their notations precisely where the movement is to take place, as actors are inclined to make their notations in the margin without indicating exactly when in the line they are to move. Another common occurrence I watch for is the tendency for actors to make the movement given them, note it in their script, and then do the line, when the intent was for them to make the movement as they speak. I always make them go back and do the movement correctly so that it goes into their memory correctly. When given a movement, the actor should note it and then make the move.

Normally I do not show an actor how to do something—a movement or a piece of business. I tell them what is needed and allow them to create how it is done. However, if I'm not being understood or the actor can't figure out how to do something, I'm not opposed to walking on the set and saying, "This is what I had in mind," and doing it for him. Sometimes that's the quickest way to get complicated action done. My good, experienced actors don't mind unless I get too specific about things that they should create—head movement, gestures, etc.

I will say here that it must be remembered that an actor is a co-creator in this process and must be allowed and encouraged to do their own work. If I start to tell an actor exactly how to move or how to say a line, then I have taken over the role and the actor is merely a puppet. I'm acting the role using his body. I must also say, that I warn the actors in advance that if they fail to do their job, I will do it for them, and they will find that it is much more fun to do what they have created than what I have created for them to do. It is far more helpful to the actor-director relationship to say, "Try making another choice," on a line reading rather than read the line for them and say, "Exactly like that." I personally wouldn't work with a director that did the latter.

During blocking rehearsals, the stage manager should be writing down the blocking in his script also. When a section or scene is blocked and we review the blocking, or when we start to work on that piece of the play, I do not want to be looking at my script to see if the blocking is correct. I want to be watching and listening. The stage manager should be following the script and has the authority to stop the actors to fix any errors in blocking.

The stage manager's note-taking also becomes helpful later if his notes include actions that influence his cue calling of the show. For example, if an actor has to turn on a light at a wall switch, the stage manager needs to note that this is a "sight cue"—one where he calls a light cue to the lighting person when the actor touches the wall switch.

Blocking rehearsals are time-consuming and not very exciting, but they are a necessary evil. The thing I try to remember during these rehearsals is not to do anything but block. Little or nothing should be done on interpretation or character development. First of all, the actor probably hasn't had the chance to study his part, and second, if I'm going to get the section blocked, I haven't the time to stop and talk about the play. That's the focus of the "work" rehearsals.

The next step is to review blocking. If time allows, it may be that same evening. Usually, it is after the entire show is blocked. During a blocking review I watch the actors, not the script, to see if what I created in my head weeks ago is still valid and is working correctly. If something is awkward or the timing of a movement does not work, I will change it then and there. Some aspects of the blocking I created may not work because of the actors I have cast. Someone may not be physically able to do what I had planned. I change it to suit the abilities of the actor. Now, on to the fun part!

Working Rehearsals.

These working rehearsals are the rehearsals where the play starts to become alive. Though the actors have not done much study yet, we start talking about what the scene or "beat" is about. We talk about relationships between the characters. We talk about what the character is thinking. We talk about nonverbal communication. We talk about the importance of certain lines. We talk about the use of the pause. If it's a comedy we are working on, we talk about how to get the laugh, the setup and the payoff , and maybe some line-delivery ideas (more about that later). What I don't deal with during early rehearsals is pace. Timing, yes. Pace, no. If we talk about pace too early, the actors have a tendency to speak too fast, not giving themselves a chance to do any of the thinking of the character. I always, always encourage actors to take their time, go slowly and give themselves a chance to find out what is in the line. The character needs to think before he speaks. I have an acting exercise I use in acting classes and rehearsals that I call "take forever." The actor is urged to take forever to get a line out. They must do all the thinking that prompts the line before they can speak. If the characters are having a conversation, they must ask and answer these questions: "What did he mean by that? How does it affect me and what I want? How do I feel about it? How should I respond?" If the questions are not an-swered aloud, an actor may fake it and pause for a long time and then say his line. I prefer to have them speak the an-swer. I often help them by doing some "side-coaching." That is, I ask them the questions and they answer and/or I help them with the answers. As one may imagine, this process takes forever and probably shouldn't be sustained too long, but it shows the actor how to create his character's think-ing—which is vital to his portrayal of the character. No line should be spoken without some thought behind it. It is easy to learn lines; it is much more difficult to create all of the thinking behind those lines. And when the thinking is cre-ated, the lines are even easier to learn. The ideal, though it is never achievable, is for the actor to think only the charac-ter's thoughts from curtain up to curtain down. The concen-tration it takes to do this is enormous and is the reason playing a large role can be exhausting.

For working rehearsals I try to schedule small sections. There is so much to do and to talk about. Trying to do a whole act early on puts too much pressure on time when we should be concentrating on what's happening in a beat or a scene. I also, as I said, try to make the most efficient use of a volunteer actor's time.

When to Start "No Books."

On my published rehearsal schedule, I indicate when actors should stop carrying their scripts. The normal time would be the first rehearsal before the week of "run-throughs." It can be a rough time with actors calling "line" every few minutes, but it must be done as soon as possible. When an actor is tied to his script, he can't do much besides read the lines. There is no eye contact with other actors, for instance. It is also difficult to deal with props with script in hand.

I have made up a rule that saves me great frustration. I learned the hard way that no guests or observers should be present at rehearsals when actors are putting their books down for the first time. This is the ugly part of the rehearsal process, and I don't want people watching my actors struggle with lines. If an observer is present, I find myself thinking, *Come on. Get that line right.* My attention is divided between the actors and what the observer is thinking. Very frustrating.

When to Start Using Props (Properties).

When actors get their scripts out of their hands is when I like to start using rehearsal props. We have probably been using some props up to then—those that are necessary for the action. But now it is time to have things that are or represent the real props. In very complicated prop shows, it is often necessary for the stage manager or his assistant to "track" props during these rehearsals. We need to make sure where certain props are at any given moment. "Is the gun on the desk or on the table? Where did you leave it?" Things of that nature.

I'm not going to stop now and talk about how to work with actors. There is a whole chapter later on entitled "Directing the Actor." For the moment my purpose is to talk about what happens in each of the different kinds of rehearsals.

Run-Through Week.

From this point on, I will be working large chunks of the play—whole acts to start with, finishing the week with a couple of run-throughs. For a two-act play, I might schedule Act I on Monday, Act II on Tuesday, possibly leave Wednesday to work on trouble spots, if there are any, and have complete run-throughs on Thursday and Friday. If everything is in pretty good shape, I may turn Wednesday's rehearsal into a run- through. If possible, the stage crew should attend at least one of the run-throughs. It will give them a good sense of what they are working on. In addition, it may be the only time they will get to see the play.

Now is the time I start working on pace and rhythm. But more about that later

For me, run-throughs are not "stop-and-fix" rehearsals. I watch and take notes. Unless there is something terribly wrong, I do not stop the actors. They need to get a sense of "playing the show." It is difficult for them to pace a beat if I keep interrupting them. I like to think, at this point, that I am an audience who talks back. I try to get an attitude of seeing the play for the first time. We run the whole act and my notes reflect what I see and hear. With the remaining rehearsal time we might go back and fix any problem areas.

I have to admit that sometimes I may not have an immediate solution to a problem. I may have to think it through and solve it the next time we do that act. The important thing is to respond to what is observed. I must trust my instincts. They're all I have.

Speaking of taking notes, I encourage my actors to have notebooks in which to write their own notes. That way, they don't have to try to remember everything I said or things they were thinking as they study in preparation for the next rehearsal. Some directors like to email their notes to their actors. Some like to write them out and hand them to the actors at the end of rehearsal. These two methods have the advantage of giving the actors hard copies of what is intended by the note. My personal feeling is that I like to look the actor in the eye to determine if he understands or if there needs to be further explanation.

Unless it is absolutely necessary, I do not schedule a rehearsal for the Saturday before Sunday technical rehearsal. It has been a long week for the cast, and they have a long, tough week ahead of them. A Saturday rehearsal would mean two straight weeks without a break. They need to rest. They also have family and "honey-dos." Remember, they are doing this for fun.

At some theatres where I have worked, they do a "cue-to-cue" rehearsal. This can be with or without actors. I personally think it is a waste of the actors' time to have them there. However it's done, this rehearsal with the stage manager and his crew can be extremely helpful in preparing for the first tech rehearsal. Without actors, I read the script and the stage manager calls the cues, which the crew execute. With actors, the actors go through the play, giving only those lines that are cues for something technical to happen.

The First Technical Rehearsal.

Some people call the first technical rehearsal "Hell Day." It is long and it is hard and it is strenuous and it is tiring. The only things missing are the flames.

In preparation for the tech rehearsal, the Stage Manager must have all the tech cues put in his book. I have been talking to the lighting and sound people. I know what is needed and where. For cues to be called on time and correctly, they have to be in the stage manager's book. I don't care how the stage manager writes his cues—there are many different ways to do it; you know—red for lights, blue for sound, "warns" the page before, etc. But the procedure is for me to sit down with the stage manager and go through the play step-by-step while he writes in the cues.

My rule number one: The technical rehearsal is not about actors. The actors are there only to do their dialogue for tech cues and to stand in the right place. This is not to say they should not do the play as rehearsed—they should—but I'm not watching their performance, I'm working with the stage manager and his crew to integrate the technical elements in to the production. Seldom, if ever, do I take an actor note during tech. I do not re-block the show during tech, even if it is the first time on the set and something is not working. I'll find some other time to do that work. There is nothing more irritating for the stage crew than to stop what they are doing and wait while the director changes the blocking. Oh, I might walk up onto the stage and say something like, "Bill, I think it might be better if you came in upstage of that drop instead of downstage. Sightlines, you know." Or, "Mary, you need to find your light for that speech." I try to keep it as simple as that. "Try" is the operative word.

I have to stop here and tell you a funny, but true story. The actors of a particular production at a major regional theatre had been working in a rehearsal room with the set taped on the floor. Rehearsing the scene, one of the characters was to turn to her right and make an exit through a door. When they moved onto the stage, with a partially completed set, this woman turned right, squatted down, and duck-waddled out through the fireplace. The door was just upstage of the fireplace. True story.

One of my jobs during tech rehearsals is to check sight lines. I go sit in a seat that is at the extreme right or left to make sure that the action can be seen by the entire audience. If there is a problem, and it is simple, I may walk down to the front of the house and motion for an actor to move slightly. If it is complicated, I take notes. I make it a practice to sit all over the theatre while I'm watching. One time I watched a scene from the balcony and realized that an actor was playing everything with his head down, looking at the floor (a common problem). I couldn't see his face. I didn't catch it rehearsing on a flat floor.

In preparation for the tech rehearsal, I always remind my actors that this is the first rehearsal for the tech people and they, the actors, should remember how good they were at their first rehearsal. No bitching, no comments are allowed from actors. One other thing, while I'm on this subject: at this point in preparation, we are building a production company. There should be no division between actors and "techies." I don't want to hear a word of criticism from either actors or techies. And, too, any social events connected with the production should include the entire company.

The technical rehearsal is run by the stage manager. I like to be on a headset, out in the audience, listening to the cues as they are called. If something is not right—a cue is missed or not called at the right time—I will talk to the stage manager and have him go back and run the cue again. (I do not talk to the lighting or sound person or a crew head. That's the stage manager's job.) It is then up to the stage manager to tell the actors and crew that we are going back and to tell everyone at what point we are starting over. He has actors wait while the tech people get ready. (In tech rehearsals, actors spend a lot of time standing around while a cue is rehearsed. Sorry. It's part of the process.) Actors should stay in their places until the stage manager tells them to "go." Do not let actors move during a blackout—it's too dangerous.

If an actor pantomimes the use of a prop and I know that prop is somewhere onstage or backstage, I will tell the stage manager to stop. He tells the actors and crew to stop and we locate the missing prop and see that the prop person knows where it is supposed to be. Sometimes the prop is off stage left when it should be right. Many times an actor has failed to get the prop from the prop table.

In complicated shows, where there are a lot of quick costume changes, these changes will have to be rehearsed. During the rehearsal, if a change is taking too long, causing an actor to miss an entrance, I will stop. (Better to miss an entrance than destroy a costume.) The costume person and I will then discuss ways of speeding up the change. Maybe the help of a "dresser" or changing something from buttons to Velcro will work. I try not to hold up the rehearsal to solve the problem. I say quick word or two and then leave it up to the costume person to figure it out. (As a side note, I strongly believe in backstage changing booths if actors have to undress down to their underwear. This is a community theatre, after all, and there is no need to embarrass anyone.) In tech rehearsals I expect the show to fall apart and look like hell. What had been finely tuned at the last run-through will be a mess. Timing will be off, lines will be dropped, people will be out of position, etc. The actors' concentration will be on other things as they get used to being on the set and in costumes. There will be constant starts and stops.

All this will have a disastrous effect. But, from experience, I know that Monday things will be better, on Tuesday we'll be closer to where we were, and on Wednesday we will be back. I have learned to trust that.

A complicated technical show may take all afternoon and all evening to rehearse. If we can get through half the show in the afternoon and the second half in the evening, then we have done what we set out to accomplish, which is to give the stage manager and his crew a chance to learn and rehearse their jobs. It's been a long, tiring day. If it gets to be late in the evening (I mean real late) and people are exhausted and grumbling, I might consider doing the final cues at the beginning of the Monday rehearsal. It's something to consider, since all my people have other lives and jobs to go to in the morning. However, waiting to do those cues will put us behind schedule. Tough it out or call it a day—it's a decision.

Monday and Tuesday I call tech and dress rehearsals. Monday we rehearse with fewer interruptions than we did the day before. If the actors didn't have costumes yesterday, they get them today. During the Monday rehearsal we try to clean up any difficult cues. If there are any blocking changes I need to make, I have the actors come in early and we fix things. Tuesday is much like Monday except that it should be running smoother. The actors normally start wearing makeup on Tuesday. Between the actor, the makeup crew, and myself, we decide what is working and what is not.

Starting with Monday and continuing through Thursday, I give the cast and crew notes after the rehearsal. I try to keep it brief because it is probably late. Depending on the number of notes I've taken, I often will write out each actor's notes and put them in the dressing room for them to read before the rehearsal. (A caution: Actors doing what was asked for in the note for the first time may be thinking about the note and not remember the subsequent lines. I've seen it many, many times.)

Wednesday, as I said before, I like to have some sort of an audience. They may be invitees of the cast and crew or maybe the theatre has invited a group. Anyone in the audience helps. If they are friends they will give great support to the production.

Thursday, final dress, I prefer not to have an audience. I want that cast and crew to be looking forward to opening night. It's magic time and I want it to be magical.

Opening Night.

Before the curtain goes up on opening night, I like to have a company meeting. The only note I might give them, if it is a comedy, is to be sure to hold for laughs (more about that in the "Directing Comedy chapter). The rest of the company meeting is thanking them for their hard work and praising them for their talents. My Stage Manager always gets special praise, as well as his crew. My opening night comments, spoken or written, always include one of my favorite pieces of direction—*"Give 'em your best."* Then I tell them to go out there and have fun.

During the opening night performance, I always like to sit at the back of the auditorium. I can take notes, and if any emergency comes up I can be easily reached. I have a little joke that I tell the cast about why I sit back there. "It's so I can get to the lobby to throw up." Polite laughter follows.

If I take notes, I do not give them after the performance. They don't want to hear them at that time. They want to be told how wonderful they were. I give notes at the company meeting before Saturday's performance. My notes should be minimal if at all. From here to the end of the run, the stage manager is in charge. Unless some drastic action is called for that he hasn't the authority to handle, it's his/her baby.

CHAPTER FIVE

DIRECTING THE ACTOR

The largest part of directing in community theatre is getting the actors ready for performance. After the preliminary work is done, we spend weeks rehearsing. The actors have to find out who their characters are, what they're thinking, and how to portray it. The task we directors undertake depends on the skill, talent, training and experience of those people we have cast. In community theatre we have to deal with performers at all levels. I have had casts made up entirely of rookies, and I have had casts where the actors have done hundreds of plays. I once had a cast of four, all of whom were directors for that theatre. I also had a cast where the first rehearsal was, "This is stage right and that is stage left." Most of my casts have been a mixture of both extremes. And I must say that I love the challenge of bringing a rookie up to the performance level of an experienced actor.

That means that the director has to be a teacher. I can imagine someone saying, "How can I teach—I've never directed before?" To that person I would say, "You must have some skills, otherwise you would not be trusted to direct the play." Obviously, some experience in acting will be useful in preparing actors. And, just as obviously, being a good actor doesn't necessarily make that person a good director. However, it is imperative that the director give actors some direction based on his/her own experience.

I once had an actor, who was about to be a first-time director, say to me, "I don't know if I'll know what to say to the actors." My answer was to really trust his instincts. We don't know everything we know. I told him to just open his mouth and start talking; he would be amazed at what came out. He would discover things about himself he never knew existed. For me, that's one of the most exciting aspects of directing—self-discovery. I'll give some direction to an actor and then I'll be thinking *Where did that come from?*

Watching actors doing a scene, I don't just listen to them. I listen to what's going on in my mind. I capture my reactions to what I'm watching and I speak. I like to say that I'm an audience who talks back. In this chapter I want to share some of what I have learned about directing community theatre actors. I will try to organize it according to problems faced or the situations encountered. I will share some of the techniques I've developed or stolen for fixing things. Some of this may seem like it belongs in an acting book instead of a book about directing, but if our job is to help actors, we ought to know something about their job.

Directing the Inexperienced Actor.

A new actor may have a spark of talent and potential to be a good actor. That's why he was cast. Unfortunately, he may have talent, but he has no craft. He knows he has to learn the lines and not fall over the furniture, but little else. Our job, then, is to teach him his job. If we want a performance from him, he has to know how to go about it. A way to start this learning experience is at the first rehearsal where I explain what my job is and what I expect from him. A new actor might think that he only has to come to rehearsal, he doesn't know how much outside study is required; or even how to study. So, I talk about that.

Creating a Character.

Well, outside of learning the lines, what is his job? He knows he's going to play a character, so let's start there. How does he find out about who his character is? First clues can be what the author gives you. Some authors, like George Bernard Shaw, will tell you almost everything you want to know. He'll even describe the shape of the character's eyebrows. Many authors will give no descriptive help at all. All the actor gets is, "He enters." Shakespeare gives no description, but it is common knowledge that everything the actor needs to know is in the lines. That means script study. I don't mean learning lines, I mean study of the play's content. (There's a wonderful story, supposedly true, that is told about two well-known actors—one young and one older. They were doing a movie together. The young actor was to play a homeless street person. So he prepared for his role by living on the streets. When the older actor questioned him about this, the young actor said that was how he prepared for his role. The older actor then said, "Why don't you just act?")

There are lots of ways to go about creating a character. So what as an actor do I study? First, I look at where the play takes place—at least the scenes I'm in. If I'm in Scene 1 and it takes place in a waterfront bar and I'm seated at the bar with another guy, it says something about me. On the other hand, if my first speech is spoken from the balcony of a beautiful home overlooking the magnificent harbor of Monaco, it says something else. The first and second guys in these examples might share some of the same qualities— they both may be honest, hardworking, contently married, and good fathers. Or they may both be the opposite— dishonest, lazy, playing around, and never see their children. What I get from the location is a sense of where my character is on the social ladder, the kinds of people he associates with, and what his daily life might be like. A starting point.

Now I look at his language. I pay particular attention to his word choices. I look at his grammar and the sophistication of the words he uses. A guy who says, "Nope, he don't," is probably not going be as sophisticated or educated as the one who says "I can, without hesitation, assure you that he most certainly does not." Might be as smart, mind you, but probably does not have the education and may not feel the need to use more words than are necessary. The guy that says, "Nope, he don't," sounds like a guy who comes right to the point and doesn't mince any words about the way he feels; it's a tough world and you'd better deal with it. He bowls and drinks beer with the guys every Thursday. The "most certainly does not" guy deals with the world using his intellect and probably has a wide range of social experiences. He likes a nice, quiet evening at home with a good book. So here is a clue to the kind of character I am— whichever one I'm playing. The more dialogue a character has, the more clues can be found about him.

What kind of situation is my character in, in terms of the action of the play? Is he attacking, or being attacked? Does he want something so bad that he is willing to do anything to get it? Or is he the person who is standing in the way of the ambitious one and is trying to prevent himself from being defeated? It may not be that obvious if I'm playing a small part; however, my character is involved in some way with the action.

What is my function? As a director, I often have to tell an actor what his character's function is. The scene in the waterfront bar may be just to set the scene for the rest of the play. The two men's dialogue may have nothing to do with the action—they may be just telling us where we are—but their job is no less hard than those of the lead characters. Look at the opening scene of Eugene O'Neil's *Anna Christie*.

If my character is the one sitting in the waterfront bar, what does he want? What are his big dreams? Maybe all he wants is a steady job, a few beers, a decent bowling average, a few laughs, and a tussle under the sheets with the old lady. His dream? "The Giants win the Superbowl." Says a lot about him and his life.

As a director, I help "no-lines" and "one-line" actors learn how to avoid being just scenery. By that I mean if an actor does not bother to create a character because he has one line

74

or no lines, then he is no different than the scenery onstage. All he does is stand there or carry in a prop. How much fun can that be? He needs to be shown how to create a character out of nothing. So I give this example: I say, "Suppose a character has the one line." The line is "Tea is served, Mum." Now, the actress playing that part could just hang around backstage until her entrance cue, come out, set the tea tray on the table, say her line, exit, then go to the pub across the street and have a beer and wait until it was time for curtain call. Every night! Boring! She'd tell her friends that she just plays a maid and only has one line. No big deal. Or she could really have some fun playing this maid if she created a character. How?

I ask the actress I'm working with, "Where does this 'Tea is served, Mum' play take place?" She answers, "England." "Describe the house," I ask. Through a series of my questions, from her imagination she describes this huge mansion, sitting on a hill outside a village. It has a grand staircase, portraits of ancestors on the walls, heavy drapes on the windows, etc. (I must admit I lead the actress down the garden path to get the some of the answers.) Now I ask, "Where does this maid live?" "In the village," is the usual answer. Sometimes it's, "In the maids' quarters." (For this example, the village works better). "Describe her house." The actress comes up with a low-class dwelling, probably upstairs over a pub with a dirty, narrow, cobblestone street in front. "What does her father do for a living?"

Answers range from running the pub downstairs to coal miner to driving a delivery truck. Then I have that actress describe the maid's father and mother. I ask her to actually see the faces. "When the maid goes to work in the morning, how does she get there?" Again, there is a range of answers: she walks, she rides her bike, she rides on the back of her boyfriend's motorbike. Any one of these is correct. But whichever one it is, it needs to be visualized.

Now, here come the most important questions. I ask, "If she has one big dream or desire, what would it be?" The correct answer (which may take some coaching) is that she would like to be the mistress of the house in which she works. "How is she going to do that?" The actress says, "By marrying the son of the present mistress," is the usual, and correct, answer.

So here we go. The actress is about to create the *SUBTEXT* for her character. If she, as the maid, enters and puts the tray down and the son is standing there, what is the maid thinking? Imagine the monologue that is going on in her head. Things like, *Oh, how handsome he looks; so proud; he's got on my favorite suit. Is he looking at me? Do I dare to make eye contact with him? Can I smile? What would be his reaction if I did? Would he smile? What would his mother do if she saw me making personal contact? Must be careful!*

Now you see, this actress could just say, "Tea is served, Mum," but there is a whole lot more going on. Maybe she gives a quick, shy glance at the son as she exits. *Did he notice me? What's he thinking?* That actress now has a character to play and that character has an environment, a family she can picture; she has dreams and desires and a way to reach her goal. Subtext! That actress gets to go to the theater every night and play this rather interesting character. What fun!

But wait! What about the son? He's carrying on a conversation with his mother and some rather dull people when this very pretty, young maid comes in with the tea. Even as he answers a question about his university, he's thinking about something else. Her. *Did she just smile at me? What did that mean? Did mother see that? I must find an excuse to see her again.* And so on.

That's how a character is created. That's the work the actor has to do. I've often had actors actually write a complete life story for their characters. It accomplishes what I just described above. If they can do the creating, then the character becomes real to them.

Creating the Character's Thinking.

We don't go to the theatre to hear actors speak words. We go to watch fully created characters *thinking* and speaking. In fact, the thinking is more interesting than the speaking. *The words are not important.* Oh, we have to say them, of course, but the play is not the words. It's what's going on in the minds of the characters.

Let me give you an example. Here are the words:

> Man: What time is it?
>
> Woman: It's eleven o'clock.

Three scenarios, using only these words:

1. Man was expecting an important visitor at ten thirty. He knows what time it is now. He's making a statement about this visitor being late. The woman's thinking, *Calm yourself. He'll be here.*

2. Man wants to know how much longer this boring lecture is going to last. Woman realizes, with pain, that it's going to last another hour.

3. The man is to go to the electric chair at twelve o'clock. *He thinks, How much more time do I have?* The woman thinks, *We only have one more hour together.*

The words are colored by the thinking of the character. The questions are asked and answered with some thought, which produces an attitude, which is expressed by the way in which the words are spoken. *The words are not important.*

There is a great scene I have been using for years in workshops. This scene can be about anything; it's called open dialogue:

A: Well, I thought you'd never get here.

B: Sorry, I was delayed.

A: Obviously. Are you staying?

B: What do you think?

A: I wouldn't know. You're such a mystery man.

B: You talk too much.

Spies? A couple breaking up? Former lovers considering reuniting? Just decide what the scene is about, put the thinking behind the words, and we have some theatre. In workshops I have sent directors off with a couple of actors each to discuss the scene. When they come back and present the scenes, the resulting performances range from violent to interesting to hilarious.

The words are not important.

Here's another way of looking at it. An iceberg floating in the water shows only, say, 10 percent above the water. The other 90 percent is below the surface. Think of the words as being 10 percent of the play—the only part we can "see." What we can't "see" is the 90 percent that is below the surface. That's where the play is. So when we study a script, that's what we are studying. Not the words on the surface, which are only a clue as to what is underneath. *SUBTEXT!*

I'm talking about directing the inexperienced actor in this section, but I want to point out, that for the director, *it is the subtext that drives the blocking.* A character may rise off the couch and cross away and say, "So, what do you think?" The reason he walks away may be because he doesn't give any importance to the response. Or he doesn't want to hear it. Or he is afraid of the answer. Whatever. If that character stays on the couch, takes a deep breath, and looks directly into the eyes of the listener and says, "What do you think?" it shows a completely different thought process. The point is, the cross or the non-cross was motivated by the thinking, not by the words.

Visualization.

If there is anything in this book worth learning, this is it!

In real life, we see directly or in our mind's eye everything we talk about. We walk outdoors, see the green grass and the blue sky, puffy clouds and bright sun, and we say, "It's a beautiful day." We see it directly. If we say, "He's disorganized, messy," we have an image in our mind's eye of this person that prompted us to say this. Both are real to us. An actor must do the same thing with his dialogue. He must visualize what he is talking about. Otherwise, it is not real to him and he is just saying the words.

Without question, the most effective directing tool I've ever used with actors is "visualization." It produces amazing results! Here's how it works: I ask the actor to visualize everything he is talking about. That's it. Well, it's not quite that simple, but that's the essence of it. I'll give you an example of what needs to be done:

This speech is from *Over the River and Through the Woods*. The character Frank is talking to his grandson:

> When I was a little boy, every Christmas morning, on the cobblestones in town, there would appear this—sea of vendors—their carts covered with toys—and what I remember most, is the colors—bright reds and blues and oranges—like a rainbow of toys. And my father would carry me in his arms and take me to the first cart, and Father would shake his head "no" and we'd move

on to the next. And I'd point to that again and again until we had gone to each cart. Then he'd buy me some little gray toy I barely wanted, and I'd start crying and he'd carry me back to our house. I always resented him for that—hated him for that. And when I was fourteen, my father put me on a boat to America and said, "Goodbye, that's where you're gonna live." I was fourteen. I hated him for that too. Not long after that, he got tangled in a fishing net that was being thrown in the water, and he hit his head on the side of the boat and they never found him. Eight years from the day he sent me away, I returned to my hometown so my mother and sisters could meet my new family. It was during the holidays, and on Christmas morning, I took your mother in my arms and carried her outside and they were there—all the vendors, like they never left—with all their blue and red and beautiful toys. And your mother pointed to the brightest and prettiest, and any one she pointed at, I bought it for her. And when we came back in, our arms full with this—rainbow of toys, my mother took one look and said: "That's what your father wished he could do! But we barely had enough to buy food on Christmas. That's why he had to send you away. So you could make for yourself a life he could never give you." I always thought my father was a bastard who wouldn't give me anything. Turns out—he was giving me all he had.

Look at all the images! Father, Christmas, cobblestones, vendors, carts, toys, colors, a little gray toy, getting on the boat, saying goodbye to family, father's death, mother, his young family, his daughter, carts, vendors, toys, mother talking to him, and a final image of his father.

Now what needs to be done by the actor, in his study, is to imagine that entire scene. Actually see every single image in that speech. Create it in his imagination. If he does that, the speech becomes real to him and, therefore, real to us. *AND HE DOESN'T HAVE TO MEMORIZE THIS SPEECH!* It's real to him—the entire story. He can tell it as though it were his own story. It's like magic! It's wonderful! If you don't believe me, read through the speech again, imaging everything as you go. See it. Then put the book down and tell the story out loud. You will be close to word perfect. If there is someone nearby as you read this, tell them the story. Don't "act it" it, just tell them the story. If they aren't entranced, I would be very surprised. I have seen this happen time and time again.

I recently did a workshop in which I used that dialogue. I asked the actor to first just read it out loud in front of the group. Then I sent him away for *five minutes* to study the speech and create his images. He came back and I asked him, to his surprise, to do the speech without looking at the book. He looked at me wide-eyed, then did the speech. He was "word perfect" and brought the group to tears. Wow!

Natural Speech.

Because what the actor is speaking is actually written, the new actor will have the tendency to speak as though it were writing. It is very "patterned."

To help the dialogue seem like it comes from thought rather than the written page, I have found some techniques that work. Not all of them work with every actor. I keep trying different ones until a light bulb goes on over his head and he "gets it."

Here are a few of them:

1. Speaking all the way to the end of the line.

Usually the most important thing we have to say is at the end of the sentence we are speaking. In real life, when we open our mouths to speak, the first few words are an introduction, but what we really want the listener to hear is at the end of the speech. In real life, we don't know what the last few words we are going to speak are going to be until we get there. To emulate real life, the actor must speak all the way to the end of the line, not knowing where the "period" is going to be until he gets there. This idea helps prevent "running down" on the end of each sentence.

2. Eliminating punctuation.

Closely associated with the above is to have the actor think about the fact that we don't, in real life, speak using capital letters, semicolons, dashes, commas, and especially periods. There is no punctuation in our speech. Using a snippet of the above dialogue, let me give an example: "...not long after that he got...tangled in a...fishing net...that was being thrown in the water and his head...hit the side of the boat and they...never found him...."

The three dots indicate where the actor might hesitate while the images come to him. But it is not the end of the sentence or even the end of the thought. Compare this with the longer speech above. Notice the punctuation is not where the hesitations I added are, and there are no caps, commas, and periods. That's the way we talk.

The "take forever" exercise I mentioned earlier helps them with this concept. I require the actor to go as slowly as possible (in rehearsal). The three dots that I just spoke of should become twelve dots or fourteen, whatever. This can do three things for the actor: it gives him time to dredge up from his subconscious the images he's describing; it allows him time to find the words to use; it gives him the chance to do something with the words. As I indicated, this is a rehearsal exercise. Once the exercise is finished, I have the actor do the speech in regular time, and what is exciting is that much of what he had created in the exercise is still there.

3. Our "bag of words."

We carry a large bag over our shoulder. The bag contains words. Our vocabulary. When we start speaking, we want the listener to understand what we are saying. And we want to find just the right words to make our point. The words are in the bag. But they are not sitting on the top. We have to rummage through the bag to find just the right words or phrase to express our thoughts. It only takes a half a second, but the point is, it *takes* a half a second. In the dialogue from *Over the River and Through the Woods,* look at all the dashes (—) in the first part of the speech. The grandfather is trying to find the words to express himself. He also probably had to find the word "rainbow." They're all in the bag. And what is really interesting, is that when we find the right word, we say it with a little more emphasis. "...like a— *rainbow* of toys."

4. *Finding the important words that carry the meaning of the speech.*

Many first-time actors make the mistake of putting the emphasis on the wrong words in their speech. If you listen closely, you hear stresses on the prepositions and connecting words like "and."

Normally, these words carry no meaning whatsoever. From the dialogue above "...It was during the holidays, and on Christmas morning..." aren't the words "holidays" and "Christmas" more important than the word "and"? Yet I find actors that will stress "and," as well as the words "the," "a," "to," and "from."

I have the actor study his lines to find the words that he uses to make his point. Then there's a little something I call, "Bringing it up out of the text." There are certain parts of an actor's dialogue that must be heard for the audience to understand: a phrase or a sentence, a "telling" line having to do with plot or theme. I suggest to the actor that he pay special attention to that part of the dialogue, to "bring it up out of the text." I don't want the actor to get corny or hammy and give it undue stress, I just want him not to gloss over something that is important to the understanding of the play.

On the other hand, there are certain words, phrases, or lines that should be unstressed or "thrown away." We often talk about "throwaway" lines in theatre. Not everything that is spoken is of equal importance or significance. In a sentence like, "Well, yes, but you do understand what's happening, don't you?" the first two words could be "thrown away"—said quickly, without emphasis. This puts even more emphasis on the important part of the line. The actor needs to decide what's important and what isn't. He may need help.

5. *Talking "to" not "at."*

Inexperienced actors sometimes have the tendency to merely quote their lines out into the air and not focus on the listener. When we speak in real life, we actually talk directly to a person to make our point, convey information, or to elicit a response. We expect some sort of reaction or feedback from the person we are talking to. Normally, we look at the listener to see if they understood what we were saying. That's what makes a conversation. Written dialogue is spoken for the same reasons. When a character speaks, he should talk *to* the listener, expecting some kind of a response. Look for it. This may mean making eye contact with them, but not necessarily. He can also listen for the response to judge whether what he has said generated any kind of understanding. But if the lines are not focused on the listener and are merely spoken, the listener may respond only by giving *their* unfocused dialogue because they did not perceive the intent of the other character.

There is an exercise that I have used with actors that have trouble making eye contact. I give them the image that the pupils of the listener are actually the holes through which what is being said gets to their brain. "Pour your intent through those holes." Let me tell you, sometimes the reaction of the listening actor is so strong it changes the dynamics between them.

I don't wish to imply that there must be constant eye contact. If you and I are talking in a room and there is no one else present, you know to whom I'm talking when I speak even if I'm not looking at you. But if I want to make an important point, I will probably look at you as I make my point to see if you understand.

6. The "Mary Had a Little Lamb" Exercise.

This one of my favorite exercises to help prevent an actor from *quoting* a speech. All the words are there, but there is no communication. So, I take that actor and sit down with him, very close, and have him tell me about Mary and her little lamb. Forget all the rhythms and rhymes. Just tell me, in a very soft voice, the story of Mary. Don't *act* it, tell me. I might even participate by interjecting my comments. For instance, after he tells me that the "fleece was white as snow," I might say, "Uh Huh." And when he tells me that "it followed her to school one day," I might say, "No kidding." We have a conversation, not a monologue or a poem. I really want to know about Mary and he really wants me to hear the story. I have found this to be very effective in helping the actor to communicate instead of quote words learned.

7. *The "What?" exercise.* I didn't dream up this exercise. I saw it used once and realized how effective it can be in breaking up speech patterns. Here's how it works: Actor "A" says his line. Actor "B" says "What?" and then Actor "A" repeats his line. Actor "B" then says his line and Actor "A" says "What?" and Actor "B" repeats his line. And so on. What happens is really interesting. When an actor repeats his line, he makes a different choice on how to say the words—a whole new line reading that usually puts the emphasis on the most important words in the speech. It makes the actor think about what the speech is about.

My experience with this exercise is that it can only be sustained for a very short time. After a few "Whats?" the actors start to find it funny and they start laughing. But used in short spurts, it is really effective. (As a side note to the "What?" exercise, I have used it in an entirely different way when I have untrained actors doing Shakespeare. Actor "A" says his line in Shakespeare's language; Actor "B" says "What?" and Actor "A" repeats the speech, this time using his own language in today's vernacular. Usually the actor gets the essence of the speech. It increases his understanding of the text. And it's fun!)

8. *Listen!*

Inexperienced actors "learn their cues." That is, they memorize the last few words of the previous speech. They listen for those words and then speak their dialogue. They don't act unless they are speaking. In normal life as someone is speaking to us, we are thinking about what they say as they are saying it. We may not speak until they have finished, but the whole time they are talking we are generating our response. That's why we sometimes interrupt people before they have finished. We need to respond to what we have just heard.

So here's the lesson for actors: *really* listen to the other actor. Think about what he is saying. Remember the four questions I mentioned earlier? "What did he mean by that? How does that affect me and what I want? How do I feel about it? In what way should I respond?" That all happens as the other actor is speaking. What he is saying and the way he says it prompts your response.

An actor can more easily learn his lines if he studies *what* is being said in the previous speeches and finds what provokes his response. Then, in rehearsal, if the actor really listens, he won't have to "learn his cues." His character's thoughts will prompt the response.

If an actor is playing a scene and he's thinking, *What's my next line?* he's in big trouble.

The one thing we hear professional actors say over and over is that the most important thing they do is listen.

9. *The head voice.*

Here's another thought on natural speech. Actors, especially new actors, tend to put on a "stage voice." They think, *We are doing dialogue here, so I had better sound like an actor.* What happens to these people is that their voices tend to leave their chests, where they talk naturally, and to go up into their heads. Men become tenors and women become sopranos. And what is really interesting is that the faster the pace, the higher their voices get. It's hard to listen to for very long. If I have an actor who has that tendency, I stop, engage him in some sort of conversation in which he needs to respond as himself, and when he does, I say, "There. That's the voice I want you to use. Get it back down in your normal speaking range, your chest voice." I can't tell you how many actors I have had to get out of their head voice. In fact, I did last night in rehearsal.

10. *The half voice.*

Another interesting thing that happens to actors, as they start to act, is that they put on what I call a "half voice." What happens is that they let air escape through the vocal chords, in the same way as when we whisper. Not all the air expelled is used to make tones. This may make their voices sound dramatic in the actor's own ears, but it doesn't do much for the audience who is straining to hear them. Full voice is needed to fill an auditorium. In film we see actors use half voice a lot. That's because the viewer and the microphone are very close to the speaker. Half voice can be very effective. Not onstage.

The Actor's Body.

Beginning actors concentrate on learning their lines and saying them correctly. They give little thought to the rest of their instrument—the body. But there is an old maxim I made up that says, "In theatre, we see more than we hear." As we watch good, experienced actors, we can tell what their characters are thinking and feeling. It's like watching a foreign film with no subtitles. We may not know exactly what they are saying, but we can tell what is going on by their actions.

If the beginning actor is not conscious of how he is using his total instrument, he may be sending the wrong visual message to the audience. Example? There is a tense situation on stage. The characters seem to be in a heated argument. But one of the actors has seated himself well back on the sofa and crossed his legs in a relaxed position. What message is the audience supposed to get from this body position? It's a heated discussion, but the one actor's body says, "I don't care." If the other actor is a female and she is sitting there with crossed ankles, how much tension are they creating for the audience? They must use their bodies to help tell the story. They need to think, again, about the total instrument.

Demonstrating. On the other hand, some beginning actors will try to tell you exactly how they feel by demonstrating it for you. Have you, ever in your life, wiped your forehead with the back of your hand when there has been a close call? No, of course not. Yet an unskilled actor might use that gesture to demonstrate that he has just survived a tense situation. As an audience, we recognize that gesture and what it means. We don't even have to know what he is thinking, he demonstrated it for us. So instead of becoming involved in the character's thinking, we watch the actor acting. Isn't that what we do when we watch a good, old-fashioned "mellerdrama?" We watch the actress playing the heroine rise up on her toes, put both hands over her heart, and flutter her eyelids when the young and handsome hero appears, and we know she loves him. Notice that I didn't say we watch the heroine do that, I said we watch the actress do that. And do all heroes have to stand chest up, feet apart, and hands on hips? Of course. That tells us who he is. We know that he is pure, brave, and honest. Again, we enjoy "meller drama" for that very reason. We love to watch the actor give all the right signals. It's the style.

If we are trying to create a sense of reality, however, this demonstrating would be embarrassing. An example: If an actor is to play a scene in which he is really angry with someone, he could pace back and forth and repeatedly slam his fist into the palm of his other hand. This demonstrates anger. But that same actor, in real life, would probably stand perfectly still, jaw tight, and tell the listener how angry he is, with his eyes.

So, I watch for actors demonstrating. I say to them, "Please don't act." Which sometimes confuses them, unless there is an explanation.

Some General Notes on Dealing with Actors.

1. Although I spend a great deal of time trying to bring the less skilled up to the level of the skilled, I constantly remind myself that everyone needs attention. I cannot ignore my best people. They need direction also. If I just let them do their own thing, and never talk to them about what they are doing or should be doing, they feel neglected. Sometimes it requires only a word or two, like, "You're right on, thank you," "You're doing a great job in that scene," or "Why don't you try..." As an actor I hate being ignored. I need to know if I'm on the right track.

2. I try to make it a point to be complimentary frequently. If an actor is constantly criticized for what he is doing, he will stop trying new things—stop making choices. He'll wait for you to tell him what to do, so it will be "right." So when he is right, he should be told.

3. I always thank the company for their work after every rehearsal. I want them to feel good about what they've done and how much it is appreciated.

4. Some new actors are intimidated by the skill of the more experienced actors. The become almost afraid of trying anything for fear of looking foolish. I watch for this and try to give them as much encouragement as possible. This brings me to a discussion of what I call, "The shell." All of us, even in our daily lives, operate within a protective shell. We seldom venture out of it to try something new. We are very comfortable and confident within that shell. We are not vulnerable. The problem is that the audience wants to see us at our most vulnerable. That's what makes us the most interesting, the most exciting. Take an actress like Meryl Streep. She certainly doesn't hide from us in her performances. She cries as well as any actress I've ever seen. She suffers, she

yells, she rages, she laughs. All of it. There is nothing about her that is held back. What she is, is what you get. And we love her for it.

I once did a production of *Who's Afraid of Virginia Woolf?* in which the young actress playing "Honey" was required to be very drunk and roll around on the floor and cry. She just couldn't let herself go to do that. She was embarrassed. One night when we rehearsed that scene, I got down on the floor with her and rolled around and cried, just as I was asking her to do. With me doing it with her, she could see that it was "acceptable behavior." After that she was fine. I'm not suggesting that we play the role for the actor. But we must find a way to help the actor break through that shell and show their vulnerability. Anything that works.

Another thing I've done with great success, is to put the problem actor at one end of the rehearsal room and I stand at the other and have that actor shout his lines. The famous director Harold Clurman, in his book *On Directing*, tells of doing this with a young, promising actor who couldn't be heard past the sixth row. Clurman went to the back row of the theater and had the actor shout his lines. Then he had him climb a rope that was hanging onstage and shout. His performance improved (forgive me) dramatically. That young actor was Marlon Brando.

5. Firing a volunteer actor is always very, very difficult. I hate it. The actor had the guts to audition, and I saw the possibility of a performance in his audition, but during the course of rehearsals, I realize he is never going to get to performance level. This can be for a variety of reasons: can't learn his lines, hasn't a clue about being onstage—you know, all that stuff. As much as I work with him, I can see that he is never going to get there Finally, for the good of the show, I have to tell him that I am going to have to replace him. I say, "John, you know, this is not working out. I have asked you to do something which is not possible for you

to do. You have tried, and tried hard. It was my mistake. I know you realize how difficult this is and I want to relieve you of the burden. I'm going to ask someone else to give it a try." Pretty corny, huh? I've only had to do it a couple of times, but that approach has worked for me. It's not him, it's me. Each time I have had to replace an actor, he felt relief, not anger. He knew he was awful and wanted out. I helped him.

I never, never, never keep an alcoholic in a cast. *Never.* I don't even try to be kind. I tell him flat out that I will not condone drinking before rehearsals or performances and, therefore, he is done.

6. I do not allow actors to coach each other. They may think they are being helpful, but if they're telling another actor how to do his part, then they are not concentrating on their own part.

7. I like actors to have a notebook in which they keep notes that I give them. When I'm in the final stages of rehearsal and we are running scenes without stopping, I take notes. At the end of a rehearsal, with all of the actors assembled, I give them these notes.

Community theatre actors are probably not going to go home after a rehearsal and study their script. It's late the next day before they have a chance to do that. Without a notebook, in which they have written what I have said to them the night before, they may have difficulty remembering exactly what I said to them.

CHAPTER SIX

DIRECTING COMEDY

Someone once said, "Comedy shows man as he is; drama shows man as he should be."

Comedy is a major staple of community theatre. In our seasons we'll have a musical and a drama and an occasional suspense play, and lots and lots of comedies. Audiences tell us they want to be entertained. To them, that means they want to laugh. Of course, a good drama is as entertaining as any comedy, but audiences buy tickets betting on the come (in gamblers' terms). If it's a comedy, they bet they are going to enjoy it. Produce a new play entitled *True Farce*, it will be a sellout. Produce the first production ever of *Death of a Salesman* and you can't give the tickets away. Who wants to go see a play about death?

Imagine this: You are doing the inaugural production of *Wit*, a play about a woman dying of ovarian cancer. If that's the story line you use in your publicity, who will come to watch this woman die? But, do the first production ever of *Noises Off* and tell your potential audiences that it is the funniest play in the English language, you won't be able to get everyone in that wants to see it. In order to survive in community theatre, we give the audiences what they *think* they want to see. There's an old joke that goes like this: Do you want to destroy a theatre? Do a season of Ibsen. (To explain the joke, in case you don't know the playwright Henrik Ibsen, who wrote, among many others, *A Doll's House, An Enemy of the People,* and *The Master Builder*, his plays are heavy on theme and the plight of his heroes and heroines against all odds. One of his plays in a season every fourth year, maybe, but an entire season? So that's the joke. Sorry to be so simplistic.)

So, back to comedy. As I said, we do a lot of it. Therefore, it would behoove us to know something about the nature of this beast. I'm not aware of anywhere one can go to study how to stage a comedy. There are probably few, if any, courses taught at the university level about playing comedy for actors or directors. Yet that is what we do most. Everywhere there are classes in voice and dance, there are classes in "I Am a Tree," in "Subtext," in "Finding Your Center," in "Emotional Recall," "In The Method," etc., but there is no one teaching "This Is How You Get This Laugh." Is the thinking that the material will do it all by itself? Despite the fact that the actor may turn upstage to deliver the punch line that's been set up, he will still get the laugh? No way. There is craft to playing comedy. It is hard work.

There's a great story, true or not, about the famous actor Edmund Kean. The story goes like this: Kean was on his deathbed and was visited by a friend. The friend said, "I'm sorry for you, my old friend. It must be difficult, dying." And Kean replied, "No. Dying is easy. Comedy is difficult." Because we have never had any formal classes in comedy, we rely on our instincts. Some of us have good instincts and some of us do not. We read a play, knowing we are going to direct it, and as we read we laugh and laugh. We say, "This is really a funny play." We don't stop at that moment to determine what it was that made us laugh. We read Neil Simon's *The Odd Couple*, for example. We laugh all the way through it.

But Neil Simon's characters don't make jokes. So what is funny?

Deciding What's Funny.

One of the first things we have to do is decide what it is that is funny about the play. There are a number of things that make us laugh; primary among these are surprise, identification, and irony. Surprise is achieved when something unexpected is done or said. The audience expects one thing and they get another.

We'll be looking at that in more detail shortly, but here's a quick example from *I Hate Hamlet:*

ANDREW: Felicia, is this how you usually operate? Séances?

FELICIA: Honey, I've been a broker for almost fifteen years. In Greenwich Village. Try human sacrifice. And cheese.

Those last two phrases are way out of context in terms of what they're talking about. We can't see them coming. The surprise of these phrases makes us laugh. (More later.)

Identification. This aspect of comedy relies on the audience identifying with something that is being done or said. "I've been there; I've done that; I've had that feeling." We get a glimpse of ourselves and subconsciously we say, "I didn't know other people have experienced or said that." Here's a quick, one-line example from *I Hate Hamlet:*

"When I go to the theatre, I sit there, and most of the time I'm thinking, *Which one is my armrest?*

Haven't we all thought that? Of course. But we didn't know other people have too. This identification makes us laugh.

Irony. This may not fit exactly the strict definition of the word, but, in theatre, I use it to mean something that is said that the audience knows, in fact, is totally opposite of what is true. The audience knows the truth; the speaker does not and we laugh because we feel superior to the characters onstage. They have no clue what is going on and we do. Irony plays a major role in many comedies, especially farce. Here's a quick example from *Noises Off:*

In fast and furious action, the telephone cradle has been thrown out the front door. The unsuspecting housekeeper, who has been misplacing everything she touches, enters from the study holding the receiver and walks to the phone table to replace it on the cradle. She starts that gesture and sees the cradle is not there. She says, "I've lost the phone now."

We laugh because we know where the phone is and she doesn't.

As a director, I try to figure out why the play is funny and how I can help the audience to find it as funny as I found it.

The Mechanics of Comedy.

Producing comedy is very technical. That is, we must know where to expect every laugh; we must know what is funny; we must know why it's funny; we most know what the audience must see or hear in order to find it funny. And then, in rehearsal, we work almost mechanically to get our results. By mechanically, I mean things like: "You need to pause, before you say that word," "Make sure the audience sees your hand come up here," "You need to do that line facing front, not profile," " Give that word a little more emphasis; it's the setup for the payoff." That kind of stuff. The director almost says, "OK, gang. This is how we get this laugh." And we rehearse it over and over until we get it just right. Of course, by then it isn't funny to us anymore.

Let me give an example of the mechanics of a setup and a payoff: In Neil Simon's *The Odd Couple* there is a dialogue sequence in which Oscar talks about a note that was left him by his roommate, Felix Ungar. He reads the note aloud and the two letters at the bottom, "FU." Those two letters could be acronyms for swear words. Those two letters are the setup, so when he continues and says, "It took me two hours to realize 'FU' meant Felix Ungar," he gets a laugh because that's not what the audience was expecting.

Now, the mechanics of the setup and the payoff: If the Oscar actor puts all the emphasis on the note and dismisses or "throws away" the "FU," the audience, if it hears it at all, will give it little attention. The result? No setup. (This is hard to do on the printed page, but bear with me.) If that actor wants to do the setup correctly, he should read the contents of the note (which are of no great importance) and then give the two letters some sort of emphasis: "F...U." Now for the payoff. As the actor does the next part of this speech, what he says at first is unimportant. The last two words "Felix Ungar," is where this dialogue is headed. To get to those last two words, the actor may increase the tempo, increase the volume, and increase the pitch, so that the line "builds" to "Felix Ungar."

If the actor fails to "build" that speech and lets those last two words get thrown away or deemphasized, the laugh will not be achieved.

A couple of other thoughts about that sequence: The Oscar actor needs to be blocked so that he takes focus (probably not in profile), and if the Oscar actor moves too much during that speech, it will be difficult for the audience to focus on what he is saying (we see more than we hear). Not that he couldn't have some movement, but too much will take focus and destroy the laugh.

The task of doing a comedy is that everything must work perfectly for it to succeed. Not true in drama. In a drama, the audience is emotionally and intellectually involved with what they are seeing. Strong dramatic moments can last for several seconds, maybe even minutes, after they have been performed. If the pace seems too slow, or an unplanned pause happens, the audience is still there, involved. Or even if a character pauses, as rehearsed, to give his character a chance to consider his reply to another character. The audience is intent on what he is thinking. They're inside his head.

But in most comedies, if that happens, you're dead. Usually, you don't want to give the audience a chance to think.

One of my favorite things to say is, "If the audience gets a chance to think, they'll realize this play isn't about anything." A late entrance, faulty cue pickup, slow pace, setup, and payoffs not heard, and things come to a screeching halt. If the audience starts to look at the scenery, we're dead.

As directors, we must pay attention to every detail. This is why the play stops being funny to us during rehearsals. We spend rehearsals analyzing it—getting it to work. When we watch a rehearsal, we are seeing that all those things we have been working on are accomplished.

Styles of Comedy.

Way back at the beginning of this book, under "Getting Started," I talked about how important it is to determine what kind of play it is we are going to be working on. It is equally important to determine what kind of comedy we have.

There are all kinds of comedies, and each calls for a particular style. If a director does not recognize the style of the play and merely treats all comedies the same, he will probably not succeed. Every style has its own characteristics and its own techniques.

Let's talk about style. There are books written on this subject that are more definitive than I will be. I am not an academic, I am a practitioner. My list of styles is limited to those with which I have to deal.

1. Slapstick

It is not uncommon for people to refer to a very funny play as "slapstick." Yet that term is grounded in history and has a specific meaning. Back in the days of the Roman Empire, comedians used a device called a "slapstick." It was shaped like a fraternity paddle and split down the middle. (When held sideways it would look something like a tuning fork.) One of the comics would be bent over, offering his behind, and the one with the "slapstick" would strike him on his rear end. The two pieces of wood coming together would make a big noise, causing great laughter. After the invention of gunpowder, the comic would put some of it in his paddle and it would make an even bigger noise, causing an even bigger laugh.

Today, though we use the term "slapstick" loosely, to my knowledge, there really aren't any true "Slapstick" plays.

There is another element of "slapstick" besides the paddle. This style uses lots of physical abuse, falling, tripping, bumping into, etc. Mostly physical humor. Are you thinking "The Three Stooges?" You're right. Know any plays like their movies? I don't.

2. Farce

I can think of no better way to introduce the subject of "farce" than quoting from an interview that Paxton Whitehead gave. Whitehead is considered to be one of the great farceurs of our time. He originated a lot of the roles in Ray Cooney's British farces, including *Run for Your Wife; Move Over, Mrs. Markham; Two into One*. He also played "Freddie" in the first production of *Noises Off*, by Michael Frayne.

Here is what he said, Read it carefully:

The best thing I could think of is that farce is about very ordinary people stuck in quite extraordinary situations. Whereas, comedy is about extraordinary people in quite ordinary situations. By extraordinary people, I mean people who are extremely witty or particularly facile—as in a Noel Coward character. You know, incredibly gifted doing quite mundane things. People in farce are not witty people. They do not make jokes. But they are squeezed into these pressurized situations and before they have time to respond rationally, they make a decision out of ignorance and then they can't put the brakes on. It's pure situation, and there has to be a good motor in farce to drive it along. If anybody stops to think—actors or audience—then everything falls apart. But you have to believe it at all times, and as an actor you have to let the audience believe that the decision you made was the logical one, at the time.

In farce, there is little or no emotional or intellectual involvement by the audience. Mostly, we are merely watching characters trying to deal with the ridiculous situation in which they find themselves. The story line is usually pretty thin, so we are not caught up in plot. The characters are so ridiculous we can't feel emotionally attached to them. There certainly is no great theme or message, so we aren't intellectualizing about what we are witnessing. We are merely watching events.

Farce is closely associated and often confused with slapstick. It is true that many of the elements of slapstick are also in farce, but the two styles are quite distinct. Both rely heavily on physical humor. In other words, the physical movements of the characters create laughter. Running up and down stairs is not necessarily funny in itself, but if a character is desperately looking for someone, or trying to avoid being seen, or trying to escape, that action can be very funny. In farce, doors open and close constantly.

I like to say, " If the curtain goes up and there are six doors on the set, it's going to be a farce. *Noises Off*, in my opinion the funniest farce ever written, has eight doors. What happens with all these doors that makes it funny? In Act I of *Noises Off*, for instance, the house is full of people running in and out of doors and they never see each other, until, eventually, they all do finally come together. In Act I alone there are 224 entrances and exits! And there are only nine characters! If even half of these entrances and exits are followed by a door slam, a cacophony of sound is created. There is one sequence where four doors slam in succession. Bang, bang, bang, bang.

Some people, mainly non-directors, find it difficult to read a farce and find it funny, because they have to imagine all of the action and the pace.

3.British Farce

There is not a lot of difference between plain farce and British farce, except that British farce normally has a lot more sexual innuendo. The British people do not discuss sexual activity as openly as we Americans. It's in their lives, certainly, but it is very private. So when the British go to see a farce by one of their playwrights they can expect to see and hear their wildest imaginings displayed onstage.

Look at a few of the titles: *No Sex, Please, We're British; Run for Your Wife; In One Bed ...And Out Another.* Someone is always trying to get someone, not his mate, into bed.

There are sexual partners hidden behind all those doors. Wives must be deceived, and the wives are often deceiving their husbands—sometimes in the same house.

Scantily clad young women scamper about the place, being chased or hidden by some man with his pants down.

The British love this.

We do too. But the Brits do it the best.

Also, British farce is often more character driven. That is, because of the nature of the characters, the action of the play happens. I look for quirks and peculiarities of the characters and play them up. Last, British farce relies less on physical humor, though the dropping of pants is a common occurrence.

4.French Farce

French farce is very similar to the two types of farce above, but to differentiate, in my experience, the French playwrights use a lot of overheard and misunderstood conversations; characters find notes they are not supposed to see, and they take the contents the wrong way. There is not as much sexual innuendo as British farce. In fact, it is often more explicit. Lots of running in and out of doors and door slams.

All farces: *LOUD AND FAST!*

5. Gag Comedy

I think gag comedy is a style of comedy that has a very narrow definition. The laughs mostly come from jokes. Granted, the characters themselves are often humorous, even clownish, but everything they say is either a setup or a payoff for a joke. I can only think of a few examples, but there probably hundreds. *Greater Tuna*, has some bizarre characters, but basically they tell jokes. An obvious example is *Sugar Babies*. The role that Mickey Rooney created for this musical is really a burlesque top banana. The dialogue is all old burlesque routines. One gag after another. When I come across one of these to direct, I make sure I understand exactly how each joke works.

6. Situation Comedy

Situation comedy is probably what we do the most. There are hundreds and hundreds of situation comedies, but an obvious example is one that I used earlier: Neil Simon's *Barefoot in the Park*. Nearly everything that happens or is spoken about has something to do with the situation in which the characters find themselves: six-flight stairway, tiny bedroom, meddling mother-in law, leaky skylight, strange neighbor. The laughs come from the characters trying to deal with the situation. That's not to say there are not some funny lines-there are. Consider this: the couple who are renting the apartment, Paul and Corie, have been out drinking ouzos (a strong Greek drink) with her mother and the strange neighbor; the mother-in-law has had too many ouzos and has to be carried up six flights of stairs. When Paul enters, exhausted from carrying her, there is a big laugh. He dumps her on the sofa. They both sit there more than a few seconds and she says, "I think my teeth are soft." Huge laugh. The situation gets a laugh and the funny line gets a laugh.

There are some other good examples of situation comedy: In *Lend Me a Tenor*, the guest operatic performer is not able to go on for his concert performance, so an inexperienced amateur is coerced into taking his place. In *I Hate Hamlet*, the situation is that a young television actor has signed a contract to play Hamlet. He is terrified and wants to get out of it. In *Over the River and Through the Woods* a young man and his grandparents are struggling with his decision to leave them and move thousands of miles away for a new job. In these, and hundreds more, the humor comes from the situation. So if, after reading the play, I've decided I'm working on a situation comedy, I play up the situation. I don't try to inject funny characters, I don't add any sexual innuendo, I don't try to make jokes. The characters trying to deal with a situation is what is funny.

7. Sophisticated Comedy

Remember what Paxton Whitehead said? I'll remind you. "By extraordinary people, I mean people who are extremely witty or particularly facile-as in a Noel Coward character. You know, incredibly gifted doing quite mundane things."

This, to me, is what sophisticated comedy is all about. And the plays of Noel Coward are the best examples. *Private Lives* is my favorite. In doing these kinds of plays, I make sure the actors realize what the style requires of their bodies. These are beautiful people. They are always conscious of how they look. They stand "just so," as if they are looking at themselves in a mirror or are about to have their photograph taken. A sit becomes a graceful, beautiful move. Men suavely cross their legs when they sit. The characters wouldn't just stand next to a piano, they would lean on it beautifully. That's what Whitehead meant by "particularly facile."

Besides the physical elements, I also look to the dialogue for the witty things the characters say. "Incredibly gifted." The wit and the physical get most of my attention.

8. Comedy of Manners

The comedy of manners requires that the audience has a certain level of sophistication. If we are going to have fun with "proper behavior," then we in the audience need to understand what is and isn't "proper." These plays make fun of society's rules of behavior in whatever time period in which the play is set. The most brilliant example of comedy of manners is, to me *The Importance of Being Earnest*, by Oscar Wilde. In this play, many of the characters are involved in situations that are not considered "proper." They are not "earnest." There is, however, one person who is steadfast in doing the right thing: Lady Bracknell, the domineering matriarch. Without that character, there would be no benchmark for "properness." The actions of the other characters would seem to be merely the actions of young people in love. We want the lovers to get together, but Lady Bracknell seems to stand in the way with her insistence on doing things according to accepted society standards of be-havior—correct "manners." If I do a play of this type, I do some research about the time period and the social struc-ture.

9. Restoration Comedy

Restoration comedy comes from the Restoration period of English history. We rarely get to work on one of these plays. They are difficult for today's audiences, so for a community theatre to do one would be really unusual. They are wonder-fully funny, but to produce one, the director has to spend an inordinate amount of time teaching his actors the style. There are books written on the subject that should be read by the director in preparation.

The plays' subject matter is not much different than that throughout history. The handsome man "A" is trying to get beautiful girl "B" into bed. But there are all kinds of compli-cations: woman "C" is trying to get man "A" into bed, but is constantly thwarted; besides she is being wooed by man "B." Girl "B" has been promised in marriage by her doctor father to his best friend's son, who is not only dumb, but ugly. There are secret meetings, overheard conversations, wily servants who lie. Not a lot of variations of plot.

Several years ago, I had the opportunity to be traveling in Spain and spent one night in a small town. When my wife and I drove into the town square, they were erecting a small stage. We asked what was happening and were told that a company from Madrid was going to be doing a play that night. After dinner, we walked out of our hotel into the square as dusk was approaching. The townspeople were gathering. The lights went on and the play started. Neither of us spoke Spanish, but instantly I knew what was going on. Every character was completely familiar: The doctor; his friend the professor; the doctor's daughter; the young, hand-some man; the drudge; the wily servants; the meddling second woman. Not understanding a word, I knew exactly what they were saying.

But here is what is important about directing this style: do the research on the period. Let me give you a couple of examples of things you would find. Everyone in that time carried a handkerchief. We've all seen plays and movies where even masculine men were waving their handkerchiefs in the air and drawing them under their noses. Also, every character, except for the servants, wears a wig. In our research we find that in those days, the people wore heavy, brocaded garments. If you look at paintings from that period, you find that most women's dresses covered them all the way to their necks. Men had high collars. Why? Because they never bathed. Their body odors were horrific. They couldn't stand their own smell. So they carried handkerchiefs, dipped in perfume, and waved them about. They wore wigs because they never washed their hair. You have to know this kind of stuff if you're going to do a Restoration comedy.

10. The Comedy of Moli'ere

Some might say this isn't really a distinct style and I would not be able to argue with them. In any case, I feel many of the plays of Moli'ere are somewhat different in that they focus mostly on the foibles of the central character. And foibles is the operative word. If you read *The Imaginary Invalid, The Doctor in Spite of Himself, The Misanthrope, The Miser* and *Tartuffe* and others by Moli'ere, I think you will find many similarities in style with those of other authors of this period, but the central character in each play is what is unique.

Therefore, if I'm doing a Moli'ere play, I start first with understanding the central character to see how he affects every other character. The other characters are wonderfully funny also, but they play in relation to the main character.

11. Satire

Webster's dictionary defines satire as "a literary genre in which ridicule is thrown upon something by stressing its worst features, often by the use of irony...and sarcasm." In dramatic literature, satirical plays normally throw ridicule on political establishments, social situations, or mores. The success of these plays depends, in a large part, upon the intellect of the audience; in order to find it funny, they must understand what it is that is being ridiculed.

Many of the plays by George Bernard Shaw are satirical in nature. Read *Arms and the Man, Don Juan in Hell, Getting Married, Major Barbara, You Never Can Tell,* and *Pygmalion* (you know that one; they made it into the musical *My Fair Lady*).

The emphasis in most satirical plays is on the dialogue. We must hear the wit of the author. Every word is chosen for its sound, its meaning, its implied meaning, and its double meaning. As the author thrusts his verbal sword into the heart of whatever it is he is ridiculing, we have to hear and understand it. Consequently, the starting place for directing a satire is to determine what is being ridiculed. This usually requires some study of the political and social situations of the time and place being dramatized.

If one looks at this list of styles, it will be noticed that from slapstick to satire there is a progression of increased reliance on the intellect and less on the physical. As directors, we must determine the nature of the beast with which we are dealing. George Bernard Shaw's characters do not slam doors and tumble over the furniture any more than Ray Cooney's characters speak insightful, intellectually challenging dialogue.

Playing Honestly.

In every style, top to bottom, the actors have to play with absolute honesty. What the characters are involved in is real and serious to them and it has to be played that way. The minute we try to "play funny," we are dead. The audience must find us funny, not watch us trying to be funny. The more serious the situation is to the characters, the funnier it will be to the audience. The character trying to escape out the window with his pants around his ankles is only funny if he must escape to avoid catastrophe. He can't be caught this way. He's not thinking, *This is a funny exit.* He's thinking, *I've got to get the hell out of here.* It's serious! We find it funny, he doesn't.

In most comedies, if not all, the audience feels superior to the characters they're watching. It's sort of like thinking, *Thank God, that's not me up there.* We watch the characters making decisions and saying things that we would never do, because we are so much smarter than they are. We would never make the decision to hide our afternoon lover in a closet when we hear our mate coming through the door. Dumb decision. Even dumber being in this situation. The mate goes to the closet to hang up a coat. We'd say, "Honey, there's something I've got to tell you..." But our character makes another dumb decision to distract the mate by lying about something, which leads to a further complication. And we feel superior.

There is another thing the audience must feel: the actors are safe, that no one will be injured. This may seem like a small thing, but there are many instances, especially in farce, where some awful things happen to characters. In *Noises Off*, for instance, one character trips over some unseen boxes on the top step of a stairway and tumbles all the way down to the stage floor and just lies there. Was it an accident or was it planned? Is he hurt or can I laugh? There is a split second when the audience doesn't know. In this particular instance, there has been so much physical activity—running up and down stairs, in and out of doors, falling over sofas—that the audience knows this has to be a planned fall. And they laugh—even applaud. The next character to speak reinforces their relief by entering, looking at the body, and saying merely, "Oh, dear."

The old "Road Runner" cartoons were funny because we knew that whatever terrible thing happened to Wile E. Coyote, he was going to be alright. When the huge boulder rolls over him and flattens him, we know he is not dead. If he were, it wouldn't be funny. But as the boulder rolls off him and we see him flattened, and then as he blows on his thumb like blowing up a balloon and snaps back into shape, it's funny. Our audiences need to feel that same sense that everything is going to be OK.

Permission to Laugh.

One final thought before we move on. I think the audience must be given permission to laugh. By this I mean that at the beginning of the play, there needs to be something that everyone will find funny so that they know it's OK to laugh out loud. I've often found that an audience will sit there *too long* before they realize that what they are watching is funny. The playwright usually helps, but if he doesn't, I try to find some amusing piece of business to get them going. Here's an example of how the author helps in the opening of Norm Foster's play *The Foursome*: (It takes place on a golf course.) Three of the four guys enter and the character of Rick "stops at the tee and bows his head."

RICK: *(He prays.)* Our father who art in Augusta, Nicklaus be thy name, thy kingdom come, thy will be done, on greens as it is in fairways.

CAMERON: What the hell are you doing?

RICK: I'm saying a prayer to Jack Nicklaus, the god of golf. Now please. Give us this day our share of birdies...

Right off, author Foster tells the audience it's OK to laugh. So that the following amusing things that are said should provoke laughter. The play is funny. It is also about the lives of four men. But what saves it from being a dreary drama about what has happened in the lives of these men is the humor. Foster wants his audience to laugh. He demonstrates that in the first speech.

Sometimes the author is of no help, so we have to create something. Let's say the first scene of a comedy begins with servants setting the dining room table. Imagine all of the things that could happen with comic possibilities: a dish discovered that is not clean; dropped silverware that is wiped on a sleeve and replaced; chairs in the wrong place; pickles from a plate that produce a "sour" reaction; a stolen kiss between servants; and on and on. This kind of action, which the director adds, tells the audience "this is going to be fun; so laugh." One of my favorite quips is "It was so funny, I could hardly keep from laughing."

Basic Elements of Playing comedy.

<u>PACE</u>

There are only two paces in comedy—fast and faster. There is no slow. (We don't want to give the audience a chance to think.) Fast and faster. Both paces are necessary. We don't want to play everything at breakneck speed (faster), because if we have one constant speed or pace that pace will, without any variety, start to seem slow because the audience gets used to it and can anticipate how the dialogue and the action will be played. It will wear on them. They will become tired of it. So we make faster even faster by contrasting it with fast. (Besides, the audience needs a chance to catch their breath.)

How do we determine what should be fast and what should be faster? A major clue is in the dialogue. Look at the lengths of the lines. A series of short speeches between characters might indicate the pace of that dialogue should be spoken very quickly or faster. On the other hand, if the characters speak to each other in long speeches (a paragraph or half a page), the dialogue may be done less quickly or only fast. This is not cut and dried, but it does give us a place to start.

Here's an example from the play *Squabbles.* Notice how during this sequence the length of the speeches starts short, then lengthens and then gets shorter and shorter, possibly indicating that the pace slows a little in the middle and then increases as it moves along to the end

A young married couple, Jerry and Alice, are childless. Her father lives with them. Alice suspects she may be pregnant from a lovemaking session they had a few months ago. She has gone to the doctor to find out and expects a phone call from him at six o'clock to tell her.

ALICE: Jer...about that night.

JERRY: Yeah? (*ALICE doesn't answer. Suddenly it dawns on him.*) Oh my God, you're pregnant. Are you pregnant?

ALICE: (*Not sure what to say.*) Well...

JERRY: (*Excited.*) Of course. You said you could get pregnant, and you got pregnant...are you pregnant?

ALICE: Well...

JERRY: Alice, if this were the Gallup Poll, you'd be entitled to a "No Opinion."

ALICE: Would you be upset if I were pregnant?

JERRY: Upset? Are you crazy? It would be terrific. We both want kids...you do want kids, don't you?

ALICE: Of course.

JERRY: *(Thinking a little levity will loosen her up.)* Whew! That's a relief. For a minute there, I thought I screwed up and married the one that didn't want kids. No...Cynthia Hackley was the one who didn't want kids. I distinctly remember, she had a Great Dane and wanted a monkey. No kids. You, on the other hand, wanted kids. No monkey. That's why I married you. It all comes back to me. *(This is not working. Frustrated, he changes direction.)* For god's sake, Alice, why would I be upset if you were pregnant?

ALICE: Well, we wouldn't have planned it.

JERRY: Alice, I promise if you're pregnant, we'll start planning right now.

ALICE: That's another giant step forward for Planned Parenthood.

JERRY: Then you're pregnant.

ALICE: I didn't say that.

JERRY: *(Humoring her.)* OK. Let's pretend you're pregnant. There are certain things we should plan. I mean, you want to keep working. We'll get a nurse...or a housekeeper. Nothing will change, except we'll have a baby... and a housekeeper.

ALICE: And, and my father. A few minor changes.

JERRY: Alice, are you pregnant? Yes or no?

ALICE: *(Reluctantly.)* Maybe.

JERRY: Maybe?

ALICE: Probably.

JERRY: *(Stating the fact.)* You are probably pregnant.

ALICE: I'm pregnant.

JERRY: You are?

ALICE: Well, I don't know for sure, but a woman knows. I'm pregnant.

JERRY: Well, sweetheart, when will you know for sure?

ALICE: Six o'clock. *(Not understanding, Jerry nods his head as if he does. Just then, the clock on the mantle chimes DONG. DONG. DONG. DONG. DONG. DONG. Jerry counts each chime patiently on his fingers. When the sixth chime rings out, he turns to Alice and smiles tenderly.)*

JERRY: Are you pregnant?

This dialogue, especially the last part, should move along at quite a fast pace as evidenced by the length of the lines.

Not all speeches can be this short. Many times a character will have lengthy speeches. In a fast-paced comedy, this can slow the pace down. Skilled authors recognize this, so they have a character interrupt the speaker with a comment of reaction or some sort of exclamation. Here is an example, again from *Squabbles:*

ABE: Do you know how my father, he should rest in peace, died? At age eighty-four he fell off a horse. And my grandfather? At the age of ninety-six, he fell off my grandmother.

JERRY: What???

ABE: I wouldn't lie. They were in a hay loft making love. He rolled over; he fell fifteen feet. Boom, he was gone.

Jerry's exclamation of "What???" in the middle of this story keeps it from being a long speech. That story could actually be told without that exclamation, but it would take longer to tell and it wouldn't be as funny.

Here's another thing that helps the pace of Abe's story: Notice how it is written in short phrases instead of long sentences. That story could have been written this way:

ABE: My father died at age eighty-four when he fell off a horse and my grandfather fell off my grandmother at ninety-six when they were in a hayloft making love and he rolled over and he fell fifteen feet and he died.

Same story. Mildly amusing. Not a big laugh. The rhythm of the speech, in short phrases, is what sets up the laugh. The final phrase, "Boom, he was gone," is what causes the big laugh because the word "Boom" comes as such a surprise.

There can be a danger in going too fast. The audience must be given a chance to hear and understand what is being said. If we're moving too fast the audience has to play catch-up. By the time they understand what is being said, the laugh line has been spoken and they've missed it. If they get it late, they won't laugh because they want to hear what is being said. We also run the danger of missing another laugh in the same line. Let's look at another sequence from *Squabbles*. Notice that the operative word is "live." It is the setup and the payoff. And there are several laughs in this exchange.

ABE: Good afternoon, Mrs. Sloan.

MILDRED: *(Surprised to see him.)* Mr. Dreyfus?

ABE: One and the same.

MILDRED: What are you doing here?

ABE: I live here.

MILRED: You're staying with Jerry and Alice?

ABE: I *live* here.

MILDRED: Jerry never told me you were visiting with them.

ABE: I *live* here. Not visiting. Living.

MILRED: How long are you staying?

ABE: It depends on how long I live. If I drop dead this afternoon, I'm sure they'll have me out of here by five, six o'clock. Seven at the latest.

If the actor playing Abe points up the word "live" in the "It depends on how long I live" line, he should get a big laugh. However, he can kill that laugh if he rushes into the second part of the line, not giving the audience a chance to "get it." As he proceeds into the second part of the line, the audience is just getting the first laugh. They will not have caught up when he does the next laugh line or the third, and all three laughs will be lost.

Another thought about pacing. Cue pickup is extremely important. Generally, if there are constant pauses between actors' speeches, the pace will slow considerably. Not to say that the deliberate use of the pause is not important—it is, and we'll discuss it shortly when we're talking about timing. However, if actors do not pick up their cues by immediately starting their speech when another actor finishes, the audience is waiting. It may seem like a small thing, but it can be deadly. I like to say that the difference between a "pause" and a "wait" is that nothing is happening in a "wait," and a "pause" is filled with thought.

One common technique for helping actors pick up their cues is to have them take the breath for their next speech on the last word spoken by the previous speaker. Experienced actors do this instinctively; the less skilled need to be reminded.

In my director's script, I indicate pace on the inside margin. I write "Fast" with an arrow under it extending down the page to where I will write "Faster" with an arrow extending down, etc. I have found that this does two things: it forces me to think about pace when I'm in the preparation stage and it reminds me when I'm in the rehearsal stage.

TIMING

Sorry. Can't be taught. You either got it or you ain't. What is timing? Here's what the Webster's Dictionary says: "1 regulation and synchronization of the various parts of a cooperative effort in order to achieve smooth performance; 2 selection of the best time to do something with the maximum effect; 3 regulation of the time or intervals of the time at which a device is to act..." All three of these definitions work for theatre timing; but I especially like the second and third, with "maximum effect" and "intervals of time."

Normally, in theatre, we mean timing to be the timed delivery of a line or a word or a movement for the maximum effect. If all of the play's dialogue is delivered as though it were coming out of a machine gun—no pauses, no hesitations, no emphasis—all the words would be heard, but it would make for a very long, boring evening. "Regulation of time or intervals of time" suggests pauses and hesitations.

Let's examine the use of the pause as a tool for timing in comedy. I'm sure you've heard Henny Youngman's famous one-line joke: "Take my wife. Please." Read that to yourself without pausing after "wife." Not funny, right? The pause after wife—-indicated by punctuation—is what makes the joke work and here is why: It is common for a comedian, in his routine, to start off a joke by saying, "Take my wife," meaning, let me tell you about her. Then he will go on and tell a funny story about his wife. Kind of like this: "Take my wife. The other day she was parking the car when..."

No pause is necessary after "wife" because he is moving on with the story and we haven't gotten to the funny part yet. Hearing "take my wife," we know what to expect. We can almost tell the rest of the story.

However, in Henny Youngman's joke he surprises us. He doesn't mean, "Let me tell you about her," he means, "Take her off my hands." We find that out when he says, "Please."

The surprise of "Please" makes a new, unexpected meaning of the word "take." The pause after "wife" has allowed the audience to go ahead of him—to keep the story going in their heads by thinking, *the other day*...How long should that pause be? I don't know. Long enough for the audience to go ahead, to be sure, but how long is that? Do I count "one" and say "Please" or do I count "One, two?" Henny Youngman probably couldn't tell us. For him, it was pure instinct.

The pause sets up surprise and surprise is what makes the audience laugh.

When I'm working with an actor, many times I will help him with pauses by telling him to put a slash in front of a word indicating to pause there. The length of the pause is up to him. If I have to have him count, I'm in deep trouble. Many times it would be just a slight hesitation. And these slight hesitations are a natural way of speaking.

Remember a while back I talked about our "bag of words"? The character may hesitate (pause) while he finds just the right word or phrase. Here is an example from *Squabbles*—Abe and Mildred have been fighting all through the play. This evening they are alone; they have just found out they are grandparents; they have opened a bottle of wine; they are sitting on the sofa when all the lights go out because of a storm; Mildred asks Abe to hold her because she is afraid; awkwardly, he puts his arm around her.

MILDRED: Mr. Dreyfus...

ABE: Yes?

MILDRED: You haven't congratulated me on becoming a grandmother.

ABE: Congratulations.

MILDRED: Mr. Dreyfus, I waited sixty-six years for my first grandchild. I think the occasion calls for a little more than that.

ABE: You want to *(A slight pause.)* shake hands?
                 (Should get a small laugh.)

MILDRED: A little more than that.

ABE: Mrs. Sloan! We're in-laws.
MILDRED: So? We're not out-laws. We're in-laws.

ABE: In-laws are natural enemies.

MILDRED: If we're natural enemies, then how come you're sitting in the dark with your arms around me?

ABE: I was thinking it could be *(Pause.)* the wine.
(Should be a good laugh. The pauses are mine, not the author's.)

"Shake hands" and "the wine" are surprises and we laugh.

I don't want to give the impression that all laughs are achieved with the use of the pause. They aren't. It is up to the actor and the director about whether to use a pause or not. Many of the best comedians do not even use a pause in their routines. They say the punch line and go right on as if they haven't said anything funny. That's what makes it funny.

Milton Berle used to give the punch line and then say, "I was..." And we laugh.

Bob Hope's technique was to do the laugh line and then say, "But I wanna tell ya..."

Jay Leno does the same thing. He does the laugh line and then says, "But, you know, folks..."

There are no finishes to those phrases. The next part of their routines do not even start with those words. They use them to allow us to laugh. They don't try to make it funny, they let us find it funny. I realize I'm talking about "gag" humor here, but the same can be true for dialogue humor.

FOCUS

This is another important element of playing comedy. The audience needs to be looking at the right place at the right time. They also must be focused on the speaker to hear what is being said. In simple terms, they must see and/or hear the setup and the payoff. If they are distracted by something—say, a movement by another character—they don't "get" the set-up and, therefore, the payoff will not get the desired laugh. In the above dialogue, suppose Mildred rearranges a pillow on the sofa just as Abe says, "the wine."

Our eye has gone to her and we don't get the impact of Abe's line.

If you're doing an important speech and someone upstage of you is eating potato chips, your speech will never be heard. To prevent this from happening, the entire cast, as an ensemble, must know where all the laughs are and what we are doing in rehearsal to make sure we get them.

I remember seeing a movie years ago where Elizabeth Taylor was behind the steering wheel of a car. The shot was through the windshield and the man sitting next to her was doing all the talking. The entire time he was talking, she was moving her fingers on the steering wheel. I never heard a word he said. She stole that scene from him.

In rehearsal we directors need to control the focus. A lot of that control comes through blocking—actor positions. In a sequence of dialogue, we need to decide what is funny and how to make sure it gets the desired laugh. If what is being said is funny, the actors should be placed so that the audience can "get" the funny line. If the reaction to what has been said is where the laugh is, the character reacting should be the point of focus.

A very simplistic example: If the line is funny, the speaker may be facing full front and the listener in profile. If the reaction to the line gets the laugh, then the speaker could be in profile and the listener facing front. *(This is not an always, merely a possible.)*

I once saw a production of a very funny play, *The Foreigner*, in which the director had staged a two-person scene with the two actors on opposite sides of the stage. My eye went to the speaking actor. As the other actor started to speak, my eye traveled over to the other side of the stage to him. By the time I could focus on him, I had missed some of what he had to say. On the other side, the first actor spoke again and I missed some of what he had to say. It was like watching a tennis match. It was interesting, but not very funny.

There are some tricks that experienced actors sometimes use to ensure that they have focus. One is to make a movement, however small, just before they speak. Our eye goes right to them because, in the theatre, movement takes precedence over sound. Another trick is to add a sound before they speak: an audible intake of breath, or adding an "ah," "uh," or "oh" to the beginning of their speech. One of my favorite "tricks" is our old friend, the pause. As a general rule, anything that follows a pause takes on extra importance. This kind of a pause gives focus to what is being said.

I must confess, not only have I used them as an actor, I have directed actors to use them. Whatever works, I always say.

DELIVERY

An actor can help himself get his laugh by the way in which he delivers his lines. Pace, rhythm, volume, emphasis, and pitch are tools the actor can use effectively.

Watch Maggie Smith work in a comedy. Many times, her voice changes slightly to help us know that what she is saying is funny. She has a little trick of delivering the funny line with a pronounced nasal twang.

The slow increase of pace, energy, and pitch during a long speech can tip off the audience that something funny is going to be said. The audience can feel the build and are ready for the laugh.

Here is an example from *Squabbles*. The *(italics)* are in the script; the *(underlined italics)* are my comments. Mildred's house has burned down, that's why she has moved in with Alice and Jerry. In this sequence Abe and Mildred are having a big fight.

MILDRED: "...I lost my house; I lost the clothes off my back; I lost every stick of furniture; I lost...*(She chokes up.)* I...lost...my bird. *(The set up.)*

ABE: *(Puffing himself up for the kill.)* Madam...

ALICE: Daddy, I know what you're going to say and don't. It's not worth it.

ABE: Don't tell me it's not worth it, Alice. I'm seventy-two years old. A straight line like that from a person like this may never come again. *(He turns to Mildred.)* So! Madam...

ALICE: Daddy, I asked you, please. *(An interrupting line which helps the pace and increases the anticipation of what is going to be said.)*

ABE: Alice, if God would come down right now, right this instant, and promise me one more opportunity like this in my lifetime, I would be glad to accommodate you. *(To God.)* Well, God? Sorry, Alice. *(He turns to Mildred, the killer stalking his victim.)* Madam *(Now here we go with the build. It starts slowly, quietly and builds in pace, volume, and intensity until the top of the build on the final word. The audience can feel it coming and are preparing to laugh.)* Madam, to look at you one would never know that you are a woman who has lost her house. One would never know that you have lost your clothes, your furniture or any of your possessions. But it has been apparent to me, from the moment you set foot in this room, that you, Madam, have lost your frigging bird!!!

Big-time payoff. Huge laugh. The line is funny, yes, but it is made funnier through the delivery.

THE ACTOR'S BODY

In addition to the voice, the body is an important part of the delivery of the comic moment. Three elements of "body" are the face, movement, and tension.

The face is extremely important in comedy. First of all, we need to see it. That sounds simple enough, but if we can't see an actor's face because of costume, lighting, makeup, blocking, or movement, we lose a focal point. We watch people's faces. We especially watch their eyes. Therefore, the eyes become very important. People who *must* wear glasses onstage are at a real disadvantage. I ask actors not to wear them if it is at all possible. Some people do not open their eyes very wide. I try to change that. Very difficult.

Too much head movement can be very destructive. It's hard to focus on someone if their head is constantly turning, twisting, and bobbing about. I watch very closely for that. I've often told an actor, "Keep your head still while you're doing that line."

Body movement can also be quite helpful in the comic moment. A full body turn or a step backwards, for instance, in reaction to someone's funny line can make the laugh even bigger. Or maybe that movement of reaction is what is funny. Part of body movement is gesture. By that I mean moving a part of the body. There are times when a small gesture can help the audience visualize the action the character is talking about. The first one that comes to mind is from a dialogue sequence we looked at before. If you recall, Abe was telling the story of his grandfather making love to his grandmother in a hayloft. When he says, "he rolled over" the actor could make a small rolling gesture with his hand, and as he says, "he fell fifteen feet," the actor could gesture slightly downward and the audience would be better able to visualize the action and, therefore, help make the laugh even bigger. Again, I'm not suggesting that every comic moment has a gesture. But as directors we want to have that as a weapon, or I should say as a tool.

TAKES

What is a take? In most instances a take is a movement in the direction of the audience to include them (to talk to them or look at them to get a reaction to something that was said); but there are other kinds as well. The important thing to remember is that takes to the audience are not appropriate in all plays. In a presentational style play, where the characters are aware that the audience is there and the audience is aware that the characters are aware they are there—that is, the characters have been directly addressing them all night—through asides about their intentions, their plans, their feelings, etc.—takes are appropriate. However, if the play is representational, representing real life, the characters are not aware the audience is there and takes are not appropriate.

There are two types of takes—those to the audience and those not to the audience.

Takes—To the Audience

1. The slow take. The actor slowly turns his entire body to face the audience. It basically says to them, "Do you believe this?"

2. The slow burn take. The actor slowly turns his entire body to the audience with a look of pain. It says, "I've never been so insulted in my life." Jack Benny, anyone?

3. The quick head take. The actor quickly turns his head to the audience with a puzzled look on his face. Essentially, this says, "Are you listening to this?"

4. The eye take. Exactly the same as the above except that the actor only moves his eyes to the audience.

5. The stop take. The actor is making a fast cross; he stops, looks at the audience, and says the funny line; he continues his cross. My favorite example of this happens in *A Funny Thing Happened On The Way To the Forum*. Pseudolous, looking for ingredients for a magic potion, makes an exit saying, "Mare's sweat. Mare's sweat. Where am I going to find mare's sweat on a balmy day like this?" A few minutes later he comes running on, stops, turns to the audience, and says, "Would you believe I found a mare sweating not two blocks from here?" He turns back and keeps on running. That's a stop take. (I have to tell you I can't do that line, even to myself, without making a slight head gesture over my shoulder to indicate where.)

Takes—Not to the Audience. These are takes that are done in reaction to something said or done onstage.

1.The double take. The reacting actor's head moves to the speaker, turns away and then, quickly, back to the speaker again. It says, "I can't believe what I just heard."

2. The over-the-shoulder take. This is a name that I have given to this reaction take. It is similar to the double take in that the reacting actor is looking at the speaker; he moves his head so that he looks over his shoulder, away from the

speaker, then turns back to the speaker before he delivers his response. The slight pause in this move brings stronger focus to what he is going to say.

3. The kick-in-the-pants take. (My name for it.) Probably used only in farce. The reacting actor is facing away from the speaker. The speaker says something surprising, and the reacting actor, as though kicked in the pants, bends his knees and goes up on his toes. (I'd love to demonstrate that, but alas...)

4. The spit take. The reacting actor takes a sip of a drink just before the speaker delivers the "surprise" line. In response to the surprise, the reacting actor spits out the drink. Again, this is such a big reaction that it is probably used only in farce.

5. The vocal take. The reacting actor takes a breath as if to speak, holds it briefly using his glottis (glottal stop), and then noisily lets the air out.

HOLDING FOR LAUGHS

I always, always remind my cast to hold for laughs. It kills me to sit in an audience and hear actors talk while the audience is laughing. The audience paid their money to come to the show to laugh. If they can't hear the dialogue because they are laughing, they will stop laughing. It's as simple as that. They may smile a lot, but they won't laugh.

Audience laughter is an interesting phenomenon. We have been rehearsing for weeks, right? We know where all the laughs are, right? *Wrong.* Audiences will do one of three things: they will laugh right where we expected them to laugh; they will not laugh where we expected them to laugh; and they will laugh where we do not expect them to laugh.

For this reason, opening nights can be a real education. You find yourself smugly say, "Yes!" when you get the expected laugh; and you say, "What wrong?" when you don't; you also say, "How did I miss that?" when they laugh in an unexpected place. OK, so we weren't perfect, we didn't see that was going to be funny; but the audience says it is.

It's that unexpected laugh that can throw actors. They're prepared to continue with their dialogue and suddenly the audience is interrupting them by laughing. So the actor says to himself, "What's funny about that?" And his concentration is gone. I have to confess, this happened to me one time. I was about to make an entrance. The onstage action was that a man was on his knees pushing up on the bra of a beautiful young woman. I opened the door and stepped onstage to view this action and the audience exploded in laughter. The director in me said "Wow, that's a funny entrance." Concentration blown, I could not think of my next line. (Fortunately, it was only for a nanosecond.)

If the audience laughs and interrupts some dialogue, it is a convention of the theatre that the actor stop, let them laugh, and then start the line over again. This implies that the actor must keep his concentration onstage, yet have an ear tuned to the audience.

The correct way to hold for a laugh is to stop, let the audience laugh, let it rise to its fullest (to its peak), and then as it begins to subside, cut it off by starting the ensuing dialogue in a voice of higher volume. In other words, we cut them off. If we wait for the laughter to diminish to nothing, it can become awkward and slows the pace.

What should an actor do while the audience is laughing? Something! To merely stand there stock still, is not natural. This may not be a problem when there is a chuckle or a short laugh, but in a long, sustained laugh, some sort of small action should take place. The actor could move about, or sit or take a drink—something. Here's a personal example from when I played in *Greater Tuna*: As Reverend

Spikes, I'm delivering a eulogy. Seated next to me is the character of Vera Carp. As Spikes delivers his boring speech, Vera Carp falls asleep and as she does she slowly lets her legs fall apart, exposing herself to the audience. The audience howls—a long, long sustained laugh. We need that laugh. I must wait for them to stop before I continue. I'm delivering a speech. I can't just stand there. What would my character do to sustain the action? I pulled a handkerchief from my coat pocket and wiped my brow, for what seemed like several minutes. If there had been water on a lectern, I might have taken a drink, or several drinks.

The point is that the play should not stop while the audience laughs. Actors need to be instructed to have some sort of business to keep the action going.

CHAPTER SEVEN

DIRECTING DRAMA

Before I begin discussing my views on directing drama, I think a couple of definitions of terms is in order. In the same way that all funny plays are not farces, not all dramas are tragedies. In common usage we may refer to a serious play as a tragedy, but the term "tragedy" refers, historically, to a specific kind of play.

To avoid being academic about this, let me quote from Webster's Dictionary: "Tragedy. A drama portraying the conflict between human will and fate or necessity, traditionally depicting a hero or heroine transcending or succumbing to, a series of catastrophic events."

To continue, Aristotle, the Greek philosopher, termed tragedy as, "The tragic hero evoked sympathy for his greatness of character but alienated it also—and caused his own downfall—by some personal flaw." By this definition, we don't see too many tragedies in modern drama. In historical drama Shakespeare presents us with some; probably Macbeth and Hamlet might be considered tragic heroes who brought about their own downfalls. In today's literature, *Death of a Salesman* has often been referred to as an American tragedy. Though not really a "hero" in the traditional sense, Willy Loman's character flaw brings about his downfall.

Drama, by definition, is "a play which, in general, is serious, not comic, but which does not rise to tragedy." This is the type of serious play we normally get to work on. There may not be a hero, in the traditional sense, in conflict with fate, overcoming or defeated by "catastrophic events," but there may be a central character or characters who are prevented from reaching their goal by other characters or events. Our hero may be an ordinary person trying to achieve something and is prevented from doing so by other forces.

So drama is conflict, conflict, conflict.

The Importance of the Story.

The most important thing to me in directing a serious play, a drama, is telling the story of the conflict. Certainly the story is essential in comedy, but normally the story is not what carries the evening. It is the laughter. If the audience "gets" the story and they are not amused—that is, they don't laugh—we have failed. In drama, if the audience doesn't "get" the story, we have failed miserably. Comedy audiences come to laugh; drama audiences come to experience a good story.

Focusing now on the story, the *storytelling moments*, which I spoke of earlier, become the most important part of script analysis. I need to know, in detail, every aspect of the story. I start by figuring out when the story begins. In many plays, if not most, the story starts before the curtain goes up. There is a history to these characters and to their relationships. There may be a situation that has existed, which may have been dormant for some time, or a conflict that has been brewing long before the play starts.

There are too many possibilities to go into much detail here, but let me give you an example from Tom Dudzic's play *Over The Tavern*. The play depicts a family in which there is considerable conflict perpetrated primarily by the father. He doesn't treat his children very well. He seems gruff and unsympathetic. It isn't until late in the play, in a story-telling moment, that we learn of an event early in the father's childhood, involving his own father, which greatly affected him. He had wanted to be a baseball player and his father broke his hand with a baseball bat. He's been bearing a grudge all these years without realizing it and taking his anger out on his children. That event caused the conflict that is now present. That's when the play started. When we, and the father, come to realize what effect that event had on him, that storytelling moment becomes extremely important and it needs to be staged so that there is no chance the audience doesn't understand.

In many plays the conflict may, indeed, start shortly after the curtain goes up. Something happens that throws the world of the characters out of balance: A man discovers that his brother is stealing from him. Or a man who owns a small company suddenly finds that he is under attack from a Wall Street type who wants to buy the company and close it for a tax write-off. Again, the first storytelling moment happens with an event that changes things for the central character or characters.

Tools to Tell the Story.

So what do I mean when I say that I pay special attention to these moments? I mean that I think about all of the tools at my disposal to help the audience:

1. The scenery.

Are there places on the stage that are more effective than others for a particular moment? For that most important speech, should I give the actor focus by placing him on a platform, or framed in a doorway, or bring him down center? Remember the example I used earlier of the king at the top of the stairway and the knight at the bottom? I'd be using the scenery to tell the story.

I use the furniture any way I can to help the audience understand. If two people are arguing and can't seem to agree on something, I may put them on either side of a table or a sofa, acting as a barrier between them. A standing person talking to a seated person usually takes focus, but not always. If the standing person is standing upstage of a sofa, for instance, we can only see part of his body, which makes him less important.

2. The lighting.

This is a tool that is often ignored by many directors: the scene starts, the lights come up to full capacity and stay that way until the scene is over. In reality, we may be able to help the dynamics of the scene by subtle light changes. Let's say there has been a big gathering of characters for a party scene and one by one they have said their goodbyes and left. The host and hostess are left alone. We have a new unit, new forces at work. An important moment in the play is coming. The audience needs to focus on what is about to be said. If, as the last guest leaves, we slowly change the lighting by taking some of the light off the walls, leaving an area, say down right, into which the host and hostess move, we give more emphasis to their conversation.

Lighting color changes can also help tell the story. It is remarkable how colors can influence an audience's feelings about what they are seeing. Unfortunately, there are not many community theaters where color changes are possible. We're usually lucky to get enough light on the stage so that the actors don't walk into "dark holes."

3. The costumes.

What characters are wearing can go a long way in helping to tell the story by telling us who they are. Colors are extremely important as they relate to character choices (the characters supposedly choose the clothes they wear in the same way that you and I do) and mood. A woman preparing to go to a party may choose to wear a black dress or a bright, gaily colored one. Her choice is going to say something about her. A change in the costuming can also help the audience. In the example used above in the lighting section, suppose that the hostess is wearing a bright, colorful party dress. We in the audience know that her frivolity is all pretense, that there is something deeply troubling her. As the last guest leaves and the lighting changes, she picks up a dark shawl and throws it around her shoulders as she walks into the lighted area. We know that what is about to be said is very important and we pay attention.

4. The sound.

This is a tricky tool to use. More often than not, I don't use recorded music to help tell the story. The decision to use it—say, for underscoring scenes or moments—depends upon the material. If a scene can be enhanced by underscoring, without calling attention to itself and without becoming melodramatic, I might consider using it. But if it is going to be used, it needs to be used throughout the production so that the audience understands that this is an element they can expect. To underscore only one scene, late in the play, would be a mistake, in my way of thinking. But consider this: If there is a great deal of underscoring,—say, in every scene—and suddenly there is none, might that not heighten that moment? As I said: tricky.

There are places where I often use recorded music, and that is between scenes. A short musical interlude as the audience sits in the dark can help in creating or sustaining a mood, which may be important to carry the audience into the next scene.

What I'm about to say has nothing to do with storytelling, but it is important. Long scene breaks are *Killers*. I strive to make them as short as humanly possible. If there is a scenery change or just a props change, the crew needs to be large enough and rehearsed enough so that they can accomplish their task quickly and not keep the audience waiting. Several things will happen if the audience is in the dark too long. First of all, we may lose the momentum we've created in the previous scene and we have to start all over again to try to get it back; second, the audience will begin to wonder if something is wrong backstage and we've lost their concentration; and third, if they sit in the dark for a very long time, they will begin to giggle. Seriously, they will. How long is too long? Lights down and lights up is ideal. Lights down for fifteen seconds is not bad. Thirty seconds is awful. If thirty seconds cannot be avoided for some technical reason, I probably would bring the house lights up so the audience can read their programs.

5. Focus through blocking.

I've already discussed this so I'm not going to go into any detail. What I want to do is to emphasize how important focus is in telling the story. We must make sure the audience is looking at and listening to that which is critical to understanding the moment. Remember: movement always takes focus. And we can use that principle to our advantage or neglect it to our disadvantage. In a scene where there are a number of characters, if all are relatively still and a character moves, however slightly, before he speaks, he takes focus and whatever he says takes on more importance.

On the other hand, if the speaker is still while others are moving about, no one will be looking at him. The importance of what he has to say will be diminished.

6. Focus through voice.

The same principles discussed in the section on comedy apply to drama as well. The pause in drama can be extremely effective in drawing the audience in to focus on the speaker. The change in pace in a conversation or even in an individual speech can help focus. Volume changes aid also. I work on these changes as I'm rehearsing. If the pace and volume and the emphasis are the same throughout the scene, nothing takes on any importance, so the audience starts to look at the scenery and the costumes and misses part of the story.

The Importance of the Characters.

The next most important thing for me to concentrate on when I'm directing a drama is the characters. The characters are the storytellers. Again, I'm not negating the importance of the characters telling the story in a comedy, but in a drama real, believable characters, fully dimensional, are of vital importance for the audience to understand why the events of the play are taking place. Drama is conflict. The characters are in conflict—in conflict with each other or with events that are taking place in their world. What puts them in conflict? Every character in a play wants something and they don't all want the same thing, and this puts them in conflict with each other. So the first thing for me to do is to decide what the central character wants. Name it: "He wants the family's fortune." That part should be relatively easy. Not so easy is the answer to the next question: "Why?"

In some plays, the answer may be obvious to the point that it is even stated by the central character. In others, it may take some digging. But dig we must, for in order for the audience to get involved in the struggle, they need to know why the struggle is so important. The fact that the central character wants the family fortune is not enough to interest us. If he wants it to become powerful in society in to order gain revenge for all the wrongs that have been done to him over the years, we now have a "why" and can understand his motives. If he is in a present state of humiliation, his desires may make him desperate. Why is it so important for him to avenge his wrongs?

In order to understand the actions a character takes in the play, the audience needs to know as much about him as possible. Hopefully, the author provides us with all the answers, but, if not, we directors must bring our own understanding of human nature to bear in our analysis—like building a psychological profile from the clues we're given. We need to know everything about him: What is his history? How did he get the way he is? What happens or has happened that has set him into action?

Authors do not write extraneous characters into their plays. Why? Because in the professional theatre, each actor receives a salary. Extra actors mean a larger payroll, which increases the investment, which makes it harder to get the play produced. So every character serves a function in the play. It is up to us, directors, to determine how each of the characters, with all their objectives and obstacles, influences the main action.

The Struggle.

Now, in terms of telling the story, I need to identify what prevents the central character from achieving his goal. What stands in his way? Who or what must he struggle with? And in the same breath—what is he willing to do in order to achieve his objective? In my "family-fortune seeker" playlet, the central character has suffered a final indignation that has enraged him. He feels if he were powerful, he could bring havoc on those who have wronged him. Since his deceased father thought him unworthy and gave the family fortune to his sister, his sister stands in his way and she is formidable. In order to win the struggle with her, he is willing to lie, forge documents, and even have his sister declared crazy and incompetent. As an audience, we sit there and watch this struggle. We may even take sides. This may seem strange to say, but in terms of the dynamics of the play, the outcome of the struggle is not as important as the struggle itself. That's what we've come to watch.

Not all plays are as simple as "a good guy against a bad guy." The struggle in the play may be broader than that. Or more obscure. If we look at *Death of a Salesman*, "good guy-bad guy" doesn't exist. The reason this play is often referred to as an "American tragedy" is that the struggle is larger than just a man; Willy Loman represents universal man; his struggle is with society. *Dancing at Lughnasa* and *The Grapes of Wrath* are plays in which whole families are struggling with societal forces that are making changes in their lives. The point is: I identify the nature of the struggle and then I try to identify the main players in the struggle. But...I do not neglect the other characters in the play, because they may have their own struggles, probably related to the main struggle.

For example, again using my "family-fortune seeker" playlet, if the rich sister has a man urging her to marry him, that man may be trying to shore up his fortunes because he has embezzled from his employer and needs to replace the money before he is found out. That's not the main struggle of the play, but his struggle influences the main action.

Audience Involvement.

If you and I were watching a football game, and just before half time the team that was behind scored a touchdown to tie the game, and I turned to you and said, "Well, let's go home," you'd think I was crazy. "That's not the end of the game," you'd say. "We've got to stay for the second half to see who wins." I say to you, "I don't care who wins, it's Cleveland and Cincinnati. I'm a Denver fan." You tell me that you're a Cleveland fan and you can't leave until you see how they do. So we watch for another hour and with two minutes to go in the game, Cleveland is down by

six points. I suggest we leave to avoid traffic. You are flab-
bergasted. "They can still win. I have to see the end." *The
end of the struggle.*

As we analyze the play we are working on, we need to
come to a realization of what it is that compels the audience
to stay and watch. Football games are easy. Dramas are
tougher. Not impossible. And some are easier than others.
For instance, we may establish a relationship during the beginning of the play with the central character and simply
want to see him achieve his goal. We don't like the opposing
forces and we root him on to victory.

An evil central character may cause us to think, *I hope he
doesn't get away with this* and we are compelled to see if he
does. I wish it were always that easy. But then we have
plays like *Death of a Salesman.* Here is the Dramatist Play
Service catalogue description of this play: "...having to do
with the last days of a failing salesman, who seeks to find
out, by a series of soul-searching revelations of the past life
he has lived with his wife, his sons and his business associates, just where and how he failed to win success and happiness." What is compelling in this story? Why do we stay to
watch it? In what way are we involved? In order to direct
this play effectively, we need to answer these questions.

I'm going to make a generalization that is often true, but
not always. Don't hold me to this. But one of the most important storytelling moments in the play often happens just
before intermission. It is common for authors to introduce a
sudden change in the situation: new information, an important new character, an unexpected action, a revelation of
intent of one of the characters. As we go out for our intermission coffee, we're thinking, *Well, well. What's this mean?*
We are compelled to come back and find out.

There is another storytelling moment that is extremely
important in terms of audience compulsion, and it also
needs to be examined closely. It is that moment in the play
when the opposing forces have thrown all their might, fired

all their ammunition, played all their cards in a desperate last attempt to win and something has to give. The action can go no further. One side must back down. *That moment needs our special attention in staging it so the audience understands what is happening and why.* If the audience leaves the theater wondering, *How could that happen? I don't get it,* we have failed. In *Death of a Salesman*, Willy Loman commits suicide. Something happens that overwhelms him. We must identify it and stage the moment so the audience understands.

Playing the End of the Play Too Soon.

Here is something else to think about. It is one of my favorite things to talk about with actors. *Don't play the end of the play until we get there.* Not one of the characters in a play knows what is going to happen. Willy Loman doesn't know he going to commit suicide. Macbeth doesn't know he's going to die. Neither of them was told in Scene 1: "You have six months to live." However, if we're not careful, our actors will play the "tragedy" of the play because they know the "tragic" ending. They'll play "woe is me" with long faces and slumped bodies. Our actors need to be encouraged to play in the present moment. If Willy Loman's meeting with his boss had gone the way he hoped it would, everything would have been fine. We would have had a different outcome to the story (and undoubtedly a different title for the play).

Hole Fixing.

Every moment of the performance should express something. Even in pauses. (A pause in which nothing is happening is a wait. Waits are bad.) We need to involve the audience every minute in some aspect of the play—intellectually, psychologically, or emotionally. If we don't, we will lose them momentarily; they are waiting for something to happen. That's when they will look at the scenery, the costumes, their programs, or their watches.

So here is something I do in the final stages of rehearsal to guard against "holes" in which nothing is being communicated. This is not easy. I try to watch a rehearsal as though I had never seen the play before. Here's the trick: Watching a scene, I make myself very conscious of what thoughts are going through my mind. The instant I start thinking about anything but what the play is saying at that moment, there is something wrong. These stray thoughts tell me there is a hole and it needs fixing.

What do I mean by stray thoughts? It can be anything: *We need to get props in the hands of the actors. Can we finish this scene before break time? Boy, she does that line well. Is this scene moving too slowly?* It takes total concentration on my part. And so to keep my concentration going, I make the briefest note possible about the hole—possibly two words of the dialogue so I know where the note comes and *maybe* a word to remind me what's wrong. If I get myself into a long "how to fix it" note at that time, I will miss too much of the play.

After the scene is over, I can look at my notes, and as I'm talking to the actors, I can come up with a solution to the problem. The alternative is to stop the actors and fix the hole right then and there. But if I'm trying to run a scene to see what shape we're in, I may destroy the momentum we've created if we stop.

There are many, many reasons for holes—too many to list them all. Here are a few so that you get the idea: the actor moving on that line takes the dramatic force out of it; those two actors are merely saying the words—quoting the dialogue—they are not involved in what they are saying; that speech is being done too fast for the audience to absorb it; this scene has been playing unrelentingly at the same pace since the beginning: the actors are not listening to each other; the actors are not acting unless they are speaking; I've put the focus on the wrong character.

In early rehearsals many of these holes are not noticed, because we are in the creative stages of developing the performance. We're more involved with the process and less with the product. When we're in the final stages, when lines are learned and most of the actors' study has been completed, and, when we're running whole sections of the play, these holes will become evident.

Rhythm, Tempo and Pace.

I'm going to lump rhythm, tempo, and pace together to try to make them easier to understand. If you would like to study these aspects of production in more detail there are many books on the subject. I think one of the best is *Fundamentals of Play Directing* by Alexander Dean and Lawrence Carra.

Let me start by saying that each motivational unit or beat should be considered almost as if it were a self-contained play with a beginning, a middle, and an end. Within each unit there are the elements of rhythm, tempo, and pace. And in putting all the units together, the entire play has all three of these elements.

Rhythm is loosely defined as the regular repetition of something. We breathe in rhythm. Our hearts beat in a regular rhythm. The beat is followed by a pause. As I write this, there is a clock on my wall that makes a clicking sound with each second. Click, pause, click, pause... But what does this mean to me as I prepare a production? I look for rhythmic possibilities in the dialogue or the movement. Let's say two people are having a heated conversation. The lines are relatively short, as each needs to express his opinion. There is the possibility of creating rhythm vocally by having one loud and one soft; or one fast and one slow; or one rough and one smooth, or one speaks instantly and one pauses before he speaks. If both stand there and forcibly argue in the same volume, pace, and tone, the conversation becomes less interesting because of the lack of rhythm. Maybe the rhythm isn't in the manner of speaking, but in the dialogue. I look for repeated ideas, phrases, or words that occur on a regular basis.

Now what is tempo? Tempo is the rate at which the beats in the rhythm occur. We still have click, pause, click, pause, but by changing the tempo, my clock could click eighty times a minute instead of sixty. There is an old theatrical trick that is used extensively in suspense films. A music underscore begins the scene with the exact same rhythmic beat as the relaxed heartbeat. As the tension in the scene increases, the tempo of the music is increased. Unconsciously, our hearts begin to beat faster. As the scene nears the scariest part, the tempo is increased to the point that we can hardly breathe, our hearts are beating so rapidly. When the moment of disaster arrives, we are prepared to react.

Okay? Now how does tempo relate to pace? (I like to think of tempo as an element of pace.) We normally think of pace as either fast or slow. But what does that mean? Here's a way to think about pace. It should be just slow enough so that the audience has time to digest what they are seeing and hearing, but not so slow that we give them a chance to become uninvolved. If it's too fast, the audience can't absorb it and they will mentally turn off the performance until they get to a place where they can get hold of it again. If it's too slow, they will wait for something interesting to happen. It's yawn and wristwatch time. There is an interesting phenomenon in the theatre. Listen next time you go to a play. At moments when the audience "checks out," you will hear a lot of coughing. On the contrary, at the highest dramatic moment, you will not hear a sound from the audience.

Let me stop here for a moment and offer some concrete examples of what I'm talking about. Let's look at two entirely different dramas: *To Kill a Mockingbird* and *A Few*

Good Men. Mockingbird takes place in a small Southern town. It is summer and it is hot. There's not much excitement in the day-to-day living of the residents. There are scenes of kids playing, scenes of people quietly talking, a scene of someone sitting on a porch swing in the evening, a scene where a housekeeper calls the kids in for dinner. The lead character, Atticus, is a lawyer and he is involved in defending a young man accused of rape. His manner is slow and methodical, even restrained. He fits right in with the way people live in this town. In fact, it is his manner that sets the pace for the play. And that pace for the most part is slow. In this play, slow pace is appropriate because what is being done and said holds the audience's attention.

A Few Good Men, a play with a military setting, probably should have a different pace. We watch young military lawyers prepare for a trial. There is a sense of urgency as they examine evidence and interview witnesses. There is growing tension as the trial nears. What the characters do is done with speed, excitement, and precision. Not every moment, but overall. This is a military court, not some small-town courtroom on a hot summer day. The pace is going to be faster. If it is paced too slowly, the audience will lose some of the tension we are trying to create in them. So pace can be influenced by the circumstances of the play.

Of the three, rhythm, tempo, and pace—for me pace is by far the most important. I have found that if I concentrate on getting the pace right in each motivational unit, the overall pace of the production will take care of itself. If we are not in control of the pace, if we don't think about it, it will take on a life of its own. Slow cue pickup, snail-paced speeches, and self-indulgent actors can kill a production.

Speaking of cue pickup, an actor can actually pick up a cue with a pause, as long as something is happening in that pause: a reaction, a movement, a long thought, etc.

And to pause or not to pause, can sometimes be the question. I once was working as an actor and at a point where my character received some stunning news, I thought the character should pause to digest this news before responding, and so that's what I did. But the director immediately shouted out to me, "Don't pause there. This is a long play." *Don't pause because it's a long play?* I uttered an oath under my breath and did as he said. Then he saw the error of his ways and said in a quiet and gentle voice, "Okay, okay, make a pause there."

A pause, in the hands of a skilled actor, can be thrilling. We love to see a character thinking. We are even drawn inside his head in an attempt to figure out what he is thinking. Consequently, we become involved in the action.

And this brings us back to *Subtext*. In an earlier section of this book, I described how subtext is created. Remember the "Tea is served, Mum" story? We heard what she said, but the character came alive when the actress created the thinking of her character. Her personal story is not in her dialogue line, it's in her thinking. In the same way, the play is not about what the characters are saying, but about what they're thinking. In other words, the play is about its *Subtext*. (The reason I italicize that word is because of its importance). Remember we are storytellers and the story being told is more than the words that are being spoken. In directing drama, more so than comedies and musicals, the *Subtext* is of prime importance.

CHAPTER EIGHT

DIRECTING MUSICALS

I sincerely hope that if you are reading this book in preparation for directing your first production, that you are not faced with doing a musical. In my view, directing musicals is the toughest and least satisfying of directing experiences. I put it in the category of herding cats: it's nearly impossible and if you are successful, it has taken every bit of your talent and energy.

Now, having said that (and frightened you considerably), let me say that there are some things to discuss that can help make the process somewhat manageable and possibly even enjoyable.

First of all, audiences do not go to a musical to hear the story. They go to hear the music and watch the dancing, never mind what it's about. Nobody hums the dialogue on the way out of the theater. As opposed to directing a drama, we are not storytellers as much as we are producers of musical entertainment. Oh, there's a story and often wonderful, meaningful dialogue, but beautiful voices singing great music and beautiful girls showing a little "T&A" (a la *A Chorus Line*) are what sell the show. So guess where we need to concentrate our directing efforts.

Even though not all musicals are musical comedies (*West Side Story,* for example), we tend to refer to any production with songs, dances, and dialogue as musical comedy. This term came into being in the early days of musicals, when the basic story line was bright, upbeat, and funny. All they really did then was to take a story line and hang a few songs and dance numbers on it. There was a formula and everyone used it. If we look at *42nd Street* and *Anything Goes,* we can see similar construction: big chorus numbers that develop into dance numbers; short dialogue scenes where the plot is advanced that end up with a solo or duet. The big number is followed by a "crossover section," which means that there is a scene in front of the main downstage drop (or curtain) while the scenery is being changed behind it. The reason it is called "crossover" is that so many of those scenes are written so that we see characters (usually a chorus) crossing from one side of the stage to another with minimal, unimportant dialogue. It's a filler until the next scene is ready.

There is a typical sequence like that in *Singin' in the Rain*. The chorus does a "crossover" on their way to see the new Don Lockwood, Lena Lamont movie. Their dialogue is about Lockwood and Lamont and completely unimportant except that it creates an excitement about seeing the new movie. The duration of the dialogue is just long enough to get the interior of the movie theater set ready. They cross over from down left to down right, the front lights dim, the drop (or curtain) goes up, and the next scene starts. At the end of that scene, the lights dim out, the drop comes in, the front lights come up, and those same chorus characters cross over from down right to down left, talking about how bad the movie was. Meanwhile, the next scene is being set up behind the drop.

Most of these conventions and formulas went out the window when a new, sensational musical opened: *Oklahoma!* They broke the mold. With the introduction of this style of musical, all of the elements were fused together. For example, dialogue led to a song, which led to a chorus entering and singing, which led to a dance number, which led to the chorus singing with the soloist, which led to the chorus exiting while the soloist finished the song, and then the dialogue continued. When that old mold was broken it was the beginning of an era when (forgive me) anything goes.

The musicals playing in the world today are so diverse that they do not fit into any formula. Rather than a formula, they may fit a category, like opera (*Les Miserables*), rock opera (*Jesus Christ Superstar*) musical drama (*Miss Saigon* and *Fiddler on the Roof*), musical comedy (*The Producers*), or singin' and dancing' musicals (*Mama Mia*). (These are categories I just made up, so don't look for an academic dissertation on the subject.)

What that means for us, directors of musicals, is that we need to determine, up front, the most important production value in the play we are about to work on. The reason I say "up front" is that some of the first decisions we have to make concern our production team. If it's an opera like *Les Miserables*, where there is minimal dancing, do I need a super choreographer or even an outstanding scenic designer? Or is the production better served with a topflight musical director and maybe a really good lighting designer?

Andrew Lloyd Webber's *The Phantom of the Opera* has been successfully staged as a concert; so how important are the visual elements in that musical? No choreographer, no scenic designer.

Now, *Mama Mia* is all about singing and dancing. Needed in the team are a terrific choreographer and a top-notch musical director.

The Producers needs a lot of scenery, and it has big dance numbers. Many of the songs can almost be spoken (like Rex Harrison as the original Professor Higgins in *My Fair Lady*). A good scenic designer and choreographer are needed for *The Producers,* and we had better reread the chapter on directing comedy.

Besides these aspects of putting a production company together, we need to think about what we are going to be looking for in auditions. If we're doing *Fiddler on the Roof*, we are looking for *actors who can act*, don't have to dance a lot, but can sing some. If it's *Phantom, Superstar,* or *Les Miz* we need to have *real singers*; acting skills are less important and they don't need to dance. For *A Chorus Line*, we need dancers, *real dancers,* who act some and sing fairly well.

Mama Mia needs *big-time singer-dancers* who can act a little. So, you see, up front we have to really study all the aspects of the production so we can decide where our emphasis is going to lie.

Oranization, Organization, Organization.

When I'm directing a comedy or a drama, organizing rehearsal schedules is fairly easy. Monday, I rehearse Act I, Scenes 1 and 2 . Tuesdays, I do Act I, Scenes 3 and 4, and so on. Musical rehearsals are much more complex and need all of my organizational skills—the reason being that there are so many divergent parts that have to be rehearsed and rehearsed in a particular order. There are also the rehearsal space requirements and the efficient use of volunteers' time to consider.

When I'm doing a musical, I have to make time for the musical director and the choreographer to do their work. With any luck and careful planning, I may be able to find a place and time to do dialogue scenes with the lead actors while the chorus is learning music or dance. But there is so much work to be done in a musical that it may be days before we get to work on dialogue. I usually give over many of the beginning rehearsals to the musical director and the choreographer to let them get a lot of their work under way. After they are under way I try to give them a big block of time several times during the week. In a musical, the dialogue often takes a backseat to all that singin' and dancin'. That's why they call it a "musical."

Depending on the musical number, actors normally have to learn the music before they can be choreographed into a dance number where they also sing. Imagine a choreographer trying to stage the musical number "One (singular sensation") in *A Chorus Line* if the dancers had not learned their music. Oh, they could work on some moves and some steps, but they would find it difficult to do any staging.

I suggest, if you need to, that you refresh your memory about scheduling rehearsals, which I discussed early on in this book. What will really be helpful in getting organized is to make that chart that says who is in which scene (and for musicals, who is in what musical number). If I have a large chorus and those characters are not named by the author, I use the actor's name. That way, I can tell which actor is supposed to be present for each part of each rehearsal. Here is an example of how complicated it can get, from *Fiddler on the Roof*: Bill, John and Mike are the three guys doing the "bottle dance" in the marriage scene. The choreographer wants to work with them, but they are also considered chorus members and the musical director needs them to learn a chorus number because two of them are in the tenor section. The choreographer will have to wait for them to finish singing; so depending on the space available, the choreographer could then take the three daughters into another room and choreograph "Matchmaker," assuming the daughters have already learned that song. While they are doing that, I can be in another space either doing dialogue with the principals or staging the song "Do You Love Me" with Tevye and Golda. This assumes the chorus is either done for the night or is on a much-needed break. I don't want them sitting around waiting.

In organizing the rehearsal schedule, I try not to do everything in the first week. For example, if there are three big dance numbers in the show, I may not schedule the start of working on the third one until the first two are pretty well done. Working with community theatre actors and performers, I have found that they like to have a sense of security about what they have accomplished thus far in the rehearsals. The best for them would be to do one number and get it to perfection and then go on to the next. The problem is, the timeline of the rehearsal schedule may not allow for a wait for perfection. They may have to start on a second number before the first is "cleaned up."

One benefit of waiting to do a number until later in the rehearsal schedule is that the choreographer may slowly come to the realization that her dancers may not be capable of doing what she had planned in that big third number. This gives her a chance to make some changes.

Let me *use Fiddler on the Roof* as an example of how the task of planning a rehearsal schedule presents itself.

1. We rehearse five nights a week for three hours each night.

2. Five weeks of rehearsal is twenty-five rehearsals. (For a musical, I like to have about twenty-eight rehearsals, from the first rehearsal to final dress.)

3. Singing rehearsals:

a. The chorus has nine numbers they have to learn to sing.
b. The principals need to learn these chorus numbers also.
c. There are ten solos and duets that have to be learned by the principals.

4. Dance rehearsals (actual dance rehearsals, with a choreographer):

a. There are four major dance numbers that take nearly the full cast.
b. There is one dance number for the three daughters,— "Matchmaker."

5. Musical numbers staging rehearsals:

a. There are four full-cast numbers that do not require a choreographer, but must be staged or blocked. (Some are simple, like "Sunrise, Sunset," where the director merely

needs to place the actors in family groups on various parts of the stage. But it still takes time.)
b. There are seven solos and/or duets that need to be staged or blocked by the director.

6. Dialogue rehearsals.

There are twenty scenes with a considerable amount of dialogue. Some scenes require the full cast; others need two or three principals.

The total of all these pieces that have to be rehearsed is *fifty-five*! And we don't rehearse things just once, do we?

Now, assuming that our production of *Fiddler* is going to open on a Friday, the preceding Sunday, Monday, Tuesday, Wednesday, and Thursday rehearsals are all technical and dress rehearsals. Hopefully, the Friday before the first technical rehearsal can be a complete, nonstop run-through. We are not learning songs, choreographing, or staging. So subtract those six rehearsals from our total of twenty-eight and that leaves us with twenty-two rehearsals, *Sixty-six hours to learn music, choreograph, and stage fifty-five pieces!* Whoa!

When you look at it that way, you can see it is a scheduling nightmare just to get everything done. If there is only one rehearsal space, it is going to take more than twenty-three rehearsals. The ideal would be to have three spaces: the rehearsal room for chorus staging and choreography, a room with a piano for music learning, and a third space for dialogue staging. Whatever the situation, the rehearsal schedule needs to be broken down into small units. That is, 7:00-7:30; 7:30-7:45; then another, 7:30-7:45 for something else. (It should only take about fifteen minutes each to stage the songs "Do You Love Me?" and "Far from the Home I Love.".) then maybe a 7:45-8:30. However, when a cast of untrained community actors are learning music and dance, they need big chunks of time.

It is almost impossible to rehearse things in sequence, and I don't even try. One night I might be staging "Sunrise, Sunset," then the dialogue preceding "Matchmaker," and next working with the actress playing Hodel on staging "Far from the Home I Love." Of course, in later rehearsals, it will become more and more possible to do things in the order in which they were written. (I remember a production of *A Funny Thing Happened on the Way to the Forum* when I played Pseudolus. We never rehearsed in sequence until we got to the first technical rehearsal. Talk about mass confusion!)

Even though the dialogue sequences have to take a backseat in the beginning rehearsals, it is important not to neglect them entirely. I sneak them in whenever I can. As the cast becomes more solid with the music and dance, I schedule more and dialogue sequences, especially those that lead directly into a musical number, because I need to make sure that the musical director and, certainly, the choreographer and I are all "on the same page."

For example, if I'm staging a dialogue sequence with two actors and I've placed them on the right side of the stage, and it turns out the choreographer has them starting the ensuing dance number at stage left, we have a problem. Or, say, in staging a previous scene I had the chorus exit stage right. They have to change costumes. The choreographer has them entering stage left for the next big number. If it were even possible, it would be a nightmare backstage. Now, realistically, this shouldn't happen, because I should have been watching the dance rehearsals and known where people were supposed be. But, through miscommunication, these things do happen and we find these things out as we start to rehearse larger and larger chunks of the play. (When I say "larger chunks," I mean, in most instances, the dialogue leading into a musical number, the musical number, and any dialogue "tag" after it.)

The upshot of this whole thing about rehearsal scheduling is to plan it out within an inch of its life.

In later rehearsals (before we go onstage), I find it very useful to have the stage manager call the cues out loud—things like "curtain up, lights up... slow fade to black... at black... spot on," etc. Normally, I have the stage crew sit in on the last few rehearsals so that they can get a feel for what it's going to be like. (Also, it may be the last time they get to see the show from the front.)

Working with the Musical Director and the Choreographer.

Earlier, I discussed production meetings with the scenic, lighting and costume designers. When doing a musical, I have to add two more artists to the team: the musical director and the choreographer. Not only do I have to work closely with each of them individually, but the three of us, together, need to get to the point where we are thinking as one person.

I'll start with the Musical Director. In community theatre, this person is normally someone from the community who has some *orchestra* experience—not just someone who plays the piano, but someone who can gather and rehearse the needed musicians. In my experience, this person is usually a music or band teacher in a local high school. I must say I have been blessed with outstanding musical directors from the teaching ranks.

The musical director is going to teach everyone—singers, dancers, and orchestra—all of the music in the show. And we're doing a musical! How important can this person be...! OK, assuming that I have found just the right person for that job, the first thing we need to do is listen to a recording of the music, if it's available, at least a couple of times. We need to discuss everything about the music: its style, its sounds, its rhythms, the images it evokes, its requirements vocally, its requirements instrumentally, the possible cuts we can make if necessary, the non-sung music (overtures, dance numbers, transitions and scene change music), everything. Now, the musical director works for me, but he is a musician, I am not. I listen very closely to his recommendations. He is a fellow artist and I rely on that input.

At auditions, the musical director can tell me whether an actor will be able to sing a role for which I am considering him. I may like an actor a lot and really want to cast him, but the musical director reminds me that the role calls for a high tenor and the actor is a low baritone. We run into this a lot in community theatre. Seldom does the perfect person show up for auditions. In the casting process there are many thing to consider. Is that actor our only choice? Is the singing aspect of this role vitally important? Can we transpose the music to a lower key? Can we rewrite some of the music to eliminate the highest notes? (Some of this will depend upon the skill of the musical director.)

Here is something else to consider: through recent developments in technology, full orchestra recordings are available for rent from the leasing companies (Music Theatre International, Tams-Witmark, etc.) for many of the well-known musicals. If a community theatre cannot afford a full orchestra with all the instruments that are required to play the score, I strongly recommend that these recordings be investigated. There are some wonderful advantages besides cost-saving. First of all, they can be used throughout the rehearsal period so that the cast can become accustomed to the sound. (This eliminates the surprise some actors have the first time they sing with a live orchestra.) Second, the recordings can be transposed into different keys. Third, and this is really cool, the tempo of the music can be changed. This means that when the actors are in the final stages of learning their music they can take it a slower pace. As they become more confident, the music can be speeded up to its normal tempo. (Unfortunately, this does not eliminate the drudgery of the early musical rehearsals when the musical director has to pound notes into the heads of non-singers.) And the ability to slow the tempo has another benefit. The choreographer can use it to teach the dance numbers at an unhurried pace, and as numbers are learned the tempo can slowly be increased until it gets to performance level. (An added benefit—the choreographer may not need the presence of a pianist at the later dance rehearsals.)

One last word about using orchestra recordings: I like to have the musical director, a pianist, and maybe a drummer in the orchestra pit during performances. Fuses blow, equipment malfunctions, the machines eat the CDs—anything can happen. I want to have a cover so that the show can go on while hair-pulling technicians try to solve the problem. It happens. Believe me. It happens.

One of the most important things the musical director and I do is plan the use of the non-sung music and the staging that may or may not accompany it. To start with, the orchestrations were written to be played for a New York Broadway production. As an example, there is music written to be played during scene changes. I might decide for my production that I cannot afford the scenery to depict a park in New York City the way it was done on Broadway. I decide, instead, to bring the lights down at the end of the previous scene, drop in a black drape (to cover the scene change into the subsequent scene), and bring on a park bench and play the scene in a pool of light. Simple and effective, but too simple for Broadway. The problem is that the orchestra score has all this music that covers an elaborate scene change. If we played it all, the audience would be sitting there waiting for the next scene to start. We don't need it all. So the musical director and I cut it to the minimum— whatever it takes to get the lights out, the drape in, the bench on, the actors on, and the lights up.

One of my favorite musical theatre phrases is "vamp 'til ready." A "vamp," in musical terms, means the repetition of a phrase or a section of music. When they're putting a Broadway production together, the composer is charged with writing just enough music to cover the scene changes. At the end of a scene, the stage manager calls his cues, technicians push buttons to make things fly in and out, lights change colors, swarms of union stagehands move scenery into place, the stage manager call his "lights up" cue, the music ends, and we are into the next scene. However, in community theatre, the stage manager calls his cues and runs to the pinrail (all those ropes that hold the flying scenery) to pull in the black, downstage drape; a volunteer grabs a rope on the pinrail and pulls out a drop, then rushes upstage and grabs another rope and pulls in another drop. Three teenagers and two senior citizens rush (?) onto the stage as the light board operator brings up the work lights. They remove the furniture and the props, and go offstage and get the furniture and the props for the next scene. At about that time, the music written for the original production would have ended. There are still things to be done: actors in place, stagehands offstage, work lights out, etc. This is where "vamp 'til ready" is used. Most often this decision happens in technical rehearsals when we discover that we need more time to change scenery. The musical director studies the score to see what phrases or sections can be repeated to last long enough for us to get the next scene ready. On the stage manager's cue, "drape up, lights up," the musical director stops the music.

Another example of non-sung music is the "play-off." In many musicals, at the end of a song or a dance number, a very short musical interlude is used to get the actors off the stage. Let's say we are just finishing a big dance number with the chorus as townspeople. They get to their big finish, some kneeling, some standing, facing the audience, arms outstretched in the "starburst" position, telling the audience to applaud; the music ends, the applause ends, and all these people need to get off the stage as the two principal actors enter and cross down center to have some dialogue. Some "play-off" music is often written to cover the chorus' exit and the principals' entrance. It is often a repeat of a phrase or two from the dance number. What is important, for me, is to stage these exits and entrances. The chorus, as dancers, are still characters in the play. If they merely stand and walk offstage the dramatic moment is lost. We see actors, not characters, exit. Those townspeople need to be going somewhere to do something. Their exits need to be motivated. In addition, the principals are coming from somewhere; they may or may not interact with the exiting chorus, but something brings them to this spot downstage center.

It needs to be staged. I cannot tell you the number of times I have seen production numbers end and the chorus just walks off. "Number over, get off the stage." Ugly!

What do I mean by, "It needs to be staged?" I'm going to make up a situation here. The chorus is in their final "starburst" position. The music ends. The applause ends. The play-off music starts, the chorus quickly crosses to the wings repeating a cute step from the dance number, and, before they exit, on a beat, they all turn back to face the audience, then step offstage. You see, it holds the audience for those few seconds until the next dialogue sequence happens.

What I've just described is called a "button." It's a device that directors create to wrap up a musical number. *It is the exclamation point!* If it can be tied in with the last note of the "play-off" music, it often evokes laughter or applause. Here's a corny example: a male actor, dressed as a woman, sings a provocative song; as he ends the song, he crosses close to the wings; he sings the last note and as he steps offstage, he looks at the audience and kicks his leg backwards in a suggestive manner, and exits. That's a button. If that number had been staged to end downstage center, that actor would have had to make an awkward cross to the wings to exit. I always look for a "button." If there is one in the music, I use it. If there isn't one, I create one. Remember, we're in show biz.

Something else I need to be conscious of during rehearsals and performances is the tempo of the music. Musical directors are usually pretty good about keeping the tempos up and bright, but they are human and concentrating on what the orchestra is playing and they may not feel the tempo begin to slow. Of course, during a performance there is nothing I can do but make a note to speak to him/her about it later.

Working With The Choreographer. This is a collaborative process that requires our best communication skills. If there is an original cast recording, together we listen to the music for the dance numbers several times. Now, I'm not a choreographer; I'm not even a dancer. I confess that I don't know many of the standard dance terms. I pretty much let the choreographer lead the way, but since I'm in charge of the production, I want to keep fairly tight control over what is going to happen, in terms of the style, the look, and the feel of a number. Together we express our ideas of what should happen in the number. I'm not shy about expressing my opinion, but I listen very carefully to his ideas. I usually speak in general terms, such as, "The music says to me that the dance is tight with short, quick movements, dancers close to each other, lots of arms." Now, if the choreographer agrees with me, he has to translate that into dance movement. As we talk, he may even get up and try some things to see if he understands what I mean, and then we talk about it. On the other hand, he may say, "You know, it sounds very Bob Fosse-ish to me" (Bob Fosse, a famous Broadway choreographer with a definite style). Even though I am familiar with Bob Fosse's style, I might say, "Show me what you mean." He then might demonstrate and say, "I see something like this or maybe some moves like this." I watch and we talk about it. In the ensuing conversation, we should be able to arrive at some decisions that will give the choreographer an approach to the dance number—an approach that will allow him/her to translate the concept into dance steps. (One thing to remember—dancing is like blocking: the audience should be able to understand what is going on even if they're deaf.)

One other thing, we discuss possible cuts in the music—cuts that will make the dancing easier. (Or shorter for the unskilled).

In community theatre, there will be many non-dancers in the chorus. The choreographer has the unenviable task of finding a way to use the entire chorus. So the trick is to keep the dances simple, but effective. The result is that the best dancers are in the front row, the less skilled behind them, and those with two left feet in the back row maybe doing only arm movements. Usually, we can cast some good, experienced dancers for the women's roles, but experienced male dancers are hard to come by. Imagine the task of teaching the male non-dancers in *West Side Story*; all young guys, with a male image to protect. Or the football team in *Best Little Whorehouse in Texas*. By the time we've been through auditions and casting, the choreographer will be able to judge what her dancers are going to be capable of. This will have a great influence on the way the dance numbers will be choreographed.

Another factor the choreographer has to be concerned about is the costumes. The time period of the play may dictate certain kinds of costumes, which could limit some of the movements he would like to use. Simple examples: high kicks mean full skirts; men in white slacks probably shouldn't do a lot of kneels; older women do not like to do upward arm movements that expose their sagging biceps. (This was learned by experience.) The point is that the choreographer and the costumer have to make sure they are on the same page.

During rehearsals, as much as possible, I try to watch dance numbers being put together. I don't necessarily watch with a critical eye; I more or less want to make sure that what we discussed is being done and also watch for any problems with blocking or entrances and exits. Rarely (but sometimes), I will make a suggestion about a particular dance step. (Sometimes I can be helpful to the two-left-feet people in the back row.)

Staging Musical Numbers.

It's obvious that musicals are different from comedies and dramas because they have music and songs, but let's take a minute to analyze why that makes them different. Songs are a poetic form of dialogue. In most musicals there is a combination of normal spoken dialogue and poetry (kind of like Shakespeare). Here's how it needs to be thought of: A scene is playing, say—two people are talking about their relationship; the more they talk, the more they become involved in expressing their feelings; when they have taken the dialogue as far as they can and there is nothing left to be spoken, they go into the poetic mode and sing about their love for each other. Songs spring from dialogue. Here is an example from *Singin' in the Rain.*

Don Lockwood (the Gene Kelly role), trying to get away from his adoring fans, meets Kathy Selden (the Debbie Reynolds role) as she waits for a trolley. He is really taken with her, but when she finds out that he's a big movie star, she gets angry and:

KATHY: You're nothing but a shadow on film—you're not flesh and blood!

DON: *(Comes toward her with a sexy, melodramatic leer.)* Oh, no?

KATHY: *(Putting up her hand.)* Stop!

DON: *(Advancing on her.)* What could I do to you? I'm just a shadow.

KATHY: *(Backing up against the bench.)* You keep away! Just because you're a big movie star—wild parties—swimming pools—you expect every girl to fall in a dead faint at your feet. *(Sitting.)* Well, don't you touch me!

DON: *(In lofty Shakespearean tone.)* Fear not, sweet lady. I will not molest you. Nay! I am only a shadow and you, my fair damsel, are but a figment of my imagination (And he sings):

> You stepped out of a dream
> You are too wonderful
> To be what you seem...

All the dialogue before the song sets up the whole idea of the song- "shadow on film...not flesh and blood...just a shadow...I am only a shadow and you...are but a figment of my imagination. Don thinks, *What's there left to say? Nothing mere words can express. So, I'll go into the poetic form and tell you more about how I feel.* (He doesn't really think that, but that's what happens).

Here is another example from the same show. (This one is so obvious it borders on corny.) It's Act I, Scene 9. Don and Kathy meet and are left alone on a sound stage. (I'll leave out the descriptive action and just use the dialogue).

DON: (I'm) so upset that I haven't been able to think of anything but you ever since.

KATHY: I've been a little upset, too.

DON: Kathy, I—seeing you again—now that I've—
Kathy, I'm trying to say something to you. But I'm such
a ham I—well I just can't do it without the proper setting.

KATHY: What do you mean?

DON: Wait a second! *(He then runs around turning on
special effects and leads her up a ladder.)* A beautiful
sunset...mist from the distant mountains...colored lights
in a garden...a lady is standing on her balcony in a rose-
trellised bower, flooded with moonlight. We add five hundred thousand kilowatts of stardust...a soft summer
breeze...and...you look lovely in the moonlight, Kathy.

KATHY: Now that you have the proper setting, can you
say it?

DON: I'll try (And he sings):

> Life was a song
> You came along
> I've laid awake
> The whole night through
> But if I dared
> To think you cared
> This is what
> I'd say to you
> You were meant for me
> And I was meant for you...

(He sings. They dance. And they fall in love.)

The song comes right out of the dialogue. Perfect.
Seldom does a character enter, walk downstage, and
start to sing. If that should be the case, the song undoubt-

edly springs from dialogue in the previous scene that sets the character to thinking, and the only way he can express his thoughts is in the poetic form. The song comes from his mind. At the end of Act I in *Singin' in the Rain,* Don does the famous "Singin' in the Rain" number. There is no dialogue in the scene. We see him taking Kathy to her apartment door, it's raining, she exits, and he begins to sing and dance. The words: "...what a glorious feelin', I'm happy again...laughin' at clouds...sun's in my heart and I'm ready for love...I've got a smile on my face...with a happy refrain..." All this comes from the previous scene (the one with the song and dance number "Good Mornin'"), when Don and Kathy solve their dilemma and fall deeper in love. The last line of the previous scene is Don's. Even though it's raining outside, he says, "Well, from where I'm standing, the sun is shining all over the place." In the blackout and scene change, Don presumably has driven Kathy home. He is ready to burst with happiness! She exits and he can't hold it back.

Now a few words about *reprise.* As the term implies, this is a repeat of a song sung previously. Often, the reprise is only part of the song; sometimes it is just a phrase or two.

What makes the reprise really interesting is that the circumstances have changed since the original song was sung. Usually (but not always), the words in the reprise then take on a different meaning. Here's an example from *Singin' in the Rain*: In Act I, Scene 6, Kathy sings the song "You Are My Lucky Star" as an audition for the head of the movie studio. At the end of the show as Kathy, embarrassed, runs out of the theatre, Don says, "Ladies and gentlemen, stop that girl! That girl running up the aisle. Stop her! That's the girl whose voice you heard and loved tonight. She's the real star of the picture. Kathy Selden!" (She stops in the aisle and Don begins to sing.) "You are my lucky star, I saw you from afar. Two lovely eyes at me were gleaming, beaming," and from the aisle Kathy sings "I was star struck." And as Don leads Kathy back up onto the stage, he sings, "You're all my lucky charms," and she sings, "I'm lucky in your arms." Of course, as they finish singing, they kiss. The reprise now becomes a real love song rather than just a song at an audition. It has real meaning.

Here's the point of all this! *Songs are dialogue* and they need to be staged (blocked) as dialogue. We need to concern ourselves with the circumstances of the play. (Where are we? What's going on? etc.) We also need to analyze the intent of the song—who is he singing to and what is the message he is trying to convey? In spoken dialogue would the speaker say, "I love you," straight out to the audience when the person he is talking to is standing at his side? I hope not. But how often have we seen this sort of thing happen in musicals—the singer sings, gloriously, but to the audience and ignores the person to whom he is singing. I'm not saying he should look at her the whole time he is singing, but there should be some sort of contact between them.

A song is like a long, spoken speech—it slowly builds to the climatic end where the point is made. There are emotional beats in the song as it grows, usually a stanza at a time; a point is expressed; the singer moves on to the next point. As his mind moves on, perhaps he should move on physically. If there is a musical bridge (a passage of music that connects two important passages, sometimes with a change of key), the meaning of those lyrics is probably a slightly different approach to what he has been singing about. If possible, I'd give him a different position on the stage.

Also, in lots of songs there are places where the orchestra plays a few phrases that have no lyrics. These are called "orchestration colorations." They are very useful to move the singer into a new area on the stage. But don't forget—something in his mind makes him move, it's not just, *Ok, here's where I cross to down left.* If the soloist is singing to someone, that person has a reaction to what is being said— she's thinking also.

Perhaps he sings something that surprises her, or disturbs her, or embarrasses her; she could move away from him which would make him follow. Just think of the lyrics as dialogue and stage it as such.

I like to do the preliminary staging without music. No piano accompaniment. I have the singer just sing/speak the lyrics slowly, making no attempt to sing full out, writing the blocking in the script as we go. At the same time, I block the other characters into the number. Once we have done that, I bring in the accompanist and we sing through it.

In terms of small movements such as gestures, body position, and head turns, I use the music. I listen carefully for any little sound in the orchestration—a drumbeat, a trill by the flutes, a trombone slide, a muted coronet doing a "wah, wah, wah." There are lots of things like that to find if I listen closely. Again, if I'm using a rented music orchestration, it makes this step much easier.

If the entire cast is onstage for a solo portion of a song that is going to end up as a big song and dance number, it seems logical to me that the solo singer should interact with the chorus. And the chorus should be given something to do besides stand there and listen to him sing. They should react appropriately to what he is singing. If they have nothing to do they are just scenery. Rather than have the soloist stand center stage and sing to the audience, he could move amongst the chorus, sing to individuals, stroll with one or two, and then when the final point of the song is about to be made, separate himself, finish the singing, and let the chorus react to what he's just said and then take over the rest of the number.

One other note about dealing with a chorus. I like to break a large chorus into groups. If I don't do that, the chorus often enters and stands in a nice, uniform semicircle. Broken into groups they can better react and interact.

It is important to remember that numbers should be staged—song and dance—as theatrically as possible. By that I mean that as a musical number progresses, it should build in energy, spirit, emotion, color, lighting effects, scenery effects—whatever—and pull out all the stops for the big finish. Make the audience applaud. This is what I call "workin' to the curtain." If the show ends with a big musical number, this "workin' to the curtain" is especially important. When that curtain comes down, you want the audience to be so excited that mere applause can not express it and they must stand to tell you how much fun they had and how much they appreciate your performance.

In this regard, let me share a story with you. A few years ago I did a community theatre production *of Anything Goes*. In it there was a production number of the song "Anything Goes." We had twenty-two tap dancers (principals and chorus) and they could flat-out dance. As the number finished, the audience stood up and applauded. It was great!

However, the way the show is written, its final number is very weak (in my opinion). It just doesn't have the theatricality of "Anything Goes." So in order to get the desired audience reaction, we put in a reprise of the big tap number—worked like gangbusters!

Technical Considerations.

There are myriad technical things that need to be dealt with. Though they are not all on the same subject, I'm going to lump them together in this section and treat each one individually.

SCENE CHANGES

Depending on the show, scene changes can be a nightmare or a breeze. Hopefully, a skilled scene designer can prevent potential headaches, but the director must take some responsibility for problems. After all, the design was created by the two of them. What can be done scenically varies from theater to theater—Is there a fly system? Is there offstage wing space for storage of scenic elements? Are rolling platforms available? Is there a drape hanging downstage that can be flown in to cover the change? Who is going to move the scenery—cast or crew? What will the budget allow? These restrictions all come into play as technical decisions are made.

Unless something is absolutely needed, I like to simplify. I mean, if I'm doing *Anything Goes,* I really need to have a two-level set depicting a ship. I also need to show a stateroom and a jail cell. On the other hand, Act I, Scene 4, in *Singin' in the Rain* is described in the script as "Hollywood Boulevard." If I have the budget, the fly system, and the building crew, I might want to paint a drop that looks like that place. However, if I need to simplify, I can merely use a bench and a trolley sign and play it in front of a drape hung upstage. This scene is not about effects, it is the start of a simple love story.

When I directed *City of Angels* I had a nightmare on my hands. The script is written like a movie script—short scenes, different locations, one after the other. We used ten-by-ten rolling platforms (four of them, if I remember correctly). Three would fit on the stage at a time, the fourth in the wings. As we moved the three to stage right, the fourth would appear from stage left. The one that was moved off into the wings stage right was redressed with new scenery. Then we'd reverse it. It took a huge crew and lots of muscle power. Tech rehearsal was aptly called "Hell Day."

Speaking of the stage crew (those are all those people dressed in black so the audience can't see them), many times a decision has to be made about whether the audience is going to see them during scene changes. Again, it depends upon the circumstances, but if at all possible I prefer not to see the crew. I realize that may not be possible, that the scene change may have to be done in full view of the audience. If that's the way it is, I try to make it as interesting and entertaining as possible. I would plan to have a low level of stage light we call "scene change light" and rehearse those changes until they can be done swiftly and with perfect precision. If a massive scene change is required (lots of stuff off and lots of stuff on), where a large crew swarms onto the stage and it must be done in view of the audience, I prefer to choreograph the movements of the crew. Done right, it can delight an audience and may even generate applause.

I try to avoid at all costs having actors move scenery in view of the audience. They are characters in a play, so when they are seen doing tech stuff, their characters are compromised. If the change is done in a blackout or behind a curtain, certainly the actors can help. And even in scene change light they can bring in a chair or bench if they are going to sit on it, and, as long as they are seated when the stage lights come up. Otherwise, for me, no actors.

The goal of scene changes is to make them as short as possible. *Thirty seconds is too long*; especially if the audience has to sit in the dark. The longer the scene change, the harder you have to work to get them back into the play when the lights come back up. It can kill a production. For me, *fifteen seconds is the maximum*. If a change cannot be done in that time, then I feel the curtain must be dropped and the house lights brought up so the audience can read their programs.

Some scene changes are held up because of costume changes. There are several solutions to this. First of all, whenever possible—Velcro, no buttons, elastic shoelaces already tied, under-dressing one costume under another. (Good costumers have more tricks than I can think of.) Second, quick-change booths offstage. Third, dressers to have the costumes ready for the actors to slip into.

Costume changes have to be rehearsed over and over to get them as fast as possible. When all else fails, have the musical director *vamp 'til ready.*

THE FOLLOW SPOT

Every director of a musical must make a decision on when to use a follow-spot. Obviously, the purpose of the spot is to center the audience's attention on the person in the light. It is very theatrical. Not every number calls for a spot. So the decision to use a spot in a number starts with asking the question, "Do I want to feature this character to the exclusion of everything and everyone else?" Probably if it is a solo and one of the lead character's "big" numbers, I would use a spot; also, if it's a duet, I would have two follow- spots. (One spot for two characters means there is not much room for movement—I don't want one of the characters walking out of the light.) If a character is featured in a number that involves many other people (like the chorus), then it is a judgment call on whether to use the spot. Generally I would not use it. If the number starts as a solo and the chorus enters, I would probably take the spot out when the chorus starts to sing or dance.

As I said, not every number calls for a follow-spot. The first example that comes to mind is in *My Fair Lady* when Henry Higgins sings, "I've Grown Accustomed to Her Face." It's a rather quiet number, reflective, he's all by himself in his study and he's talking aloud to himself. It's charming. To suddenly throw a follow-spot on him would, in my opinion, make the number much more "show bizy" and destroy the mood. There are a couple of possible options, however. If the follow-spot equipment has the ability to give a soft edge to the light, I might consider sneaking it in and taking the rest of the stage level light down a bit. Or, if he going to sing this song without moving too much, I might want to hang a special light and when the music introduction of the song starts, take the area light down a bit and leave the special for him to sing in.

On the other hand, when Tevya sings, "If I Were a Rich Man," in *Fiddler on the Roof*, he is by himself, talking to himself, but the number is up, bright, with considerable comic energy, and I would definitely use a follow-spot.

There's no hard and fast rule, and every show has its own decisions to be made.

LIGHTING

Hopefully, I've got a good lighting designer who has done musicals before. But, in community theatre, this is not always the case. So here are a few of my guidelines when I'm dealing with an inexperienced designer:

1. If you can't see, you can't hear! (True for any kind of show.)

2. More light! (The more energy in a number, the brighter the stage.)

3. Don't be afraid to use some colors in the big numbers.

4. Side lighting in dance numbers adds dimension to dancers' bodies.

5. Don't light areas of the stage that are not in use or are not going to be used.

6. Avoid too many internal (within the scene) light changes-level up, level down, level up, level down...

7. The length of a fade to black at the end of a number depends upon the energy of the number—more energy

means faster fade and vice versa. (An example: sweet love song—slow fade to black).

TO MIC OR NOT TO MIC

I prefer not to put *head mics* on actors. I have and I will in the future, but I really would not choose to do it. A couple of reasons: I think it changes the intimacy of the theatre. We go to the movies and we hear amplified sound and it puts a distance between the actors and ourselves. One of the great things about theatre is the close bond between the actor and the audience. I think when we mic, we lose that. Miking also can change the tone in the singing voice. In addition to those considerations is the fact that adding microphones adds headaches: mics fail, batteries fail, volume controls are subject to operator error. If it can go wrong, it will. A head mic requires a battery pack that needs to be hidden in the costume. It also means that there is something sticking out of the actor's hair that needs to be disguised as much as possible.

Now, there are some shows where amplified sound is needed. Most of the rock musicals are written so that the orchestra must play very loudly in order to achieve the desired sound. A singing voice would be unheard unless it was amplified. It is necessary to get the voice "up, over" the orchestra, and so head-mics are not only justified, but required.

If at all possible, I would make the choice to use "floor mics" downstage or possibly overhead hanging-mics. But the rule is—if they can't hear it, they will hate it. Judgment call.

PUTTING IT ALL TOGETHER

As I said at the beginning of this chapter, directing a musical is hard work. It takes all the energy, perseverance, patience, tact, luck, theatre instinct, and talent a director can muster. In the first few rehearsals you think "we're never going to get there." There are so many things that are happening that are under someone else's control—the music, dances, sets, lights, props, costumes—it's difficult to get a good grip on how you're coming along. I'll see a friend on the street and they'll ask, "How's the show comin'?" and I'll say something like, "Oh, we're gettin' there." I absolutely cannot be more specific than that. (My mother, a professional actress, once told me, "Don't worry. When opening night comes, the curtain will go up." Yeah. Thanks, Mom.) It isn't until the later rehearsals, when it starts to come together that I can get a handle on where we are in the process. When the music, dances, and dialogue are learned, numbers are staged, sets are constructed, and costumes are being fitted, then I can answer that question by saying, "It's really coming together. I think we're going to be OK."

In the latter stages of rehearsal, more of the responsibility for the quality of the show falls on me. I need to take all the pieces and put them together. I start putting dialogue and songs together, working with the actors to make sure they understand how the song they've learned comes out of the dialogue, and then how that moves into dance, more song, and maybe more dialogue. The chorus has learned their music and their dance numbers, but they have no idea how they fit into the action of the play. For instance, I may have been rehearsing dialogue with the leads and now I bring in the chorus people that are onstage during this sequence. They need to find out who they are in the scene: "Where am I supposed to be? How do I get there? What is my attitude? To whom do I relate, both physically and emotionally? What should be the size of my performance? When the scene is over, where do I go?"

In Act I, Scene 4, of *Singin' in the Rain,* it says in the script, "Hollywood Boulevard. Night. There are people strolling."

Those people who are "strolling" are the chorus members who are going to sing, *You Stepped Out of a Dream"* later in this scene. There are a number of things to deal with here: where do the people stroll from and where are they going?

There is dialogue going on between Don and Kathy downstage around the bench so the chorus cannot be too distracting. They probably enter from offstage right and left and they exit right and left. How many at a time? Maybe two lovers from right, arm in arm, and they are crossed by four girls from stage left. The four from left may linger a moment to have a pantomimed conversation before they exit. Then two more from left who are reading a city map and, as they exit, three from stage right. Whatever, seems natural. Now, who are these people and why are they out strolling? Some might be sightseers visiting Hollywood. Some might be shoppers. (A babe and her sugar daddy cross left to right, and later they cross right to left with him following her with a stack of packages.) One group might be a mother holding the hands of her two children. Maybe someone could cross riding a bike. The point is that each chorus member should be given a character to play in the scene. Each character has a reason to be there. They've been somewhere and they're going somewhere. They also have an attitude about what they're doing. Again, if the director and actors don't create that, the actors are just scenery.

Here's an example from Act I, Scene 4, in *Fiddler on the Roof.* (This is the scene in which Tevye agrees to match his daughter with the butcher, Lazar Wolf.) The description says, "The inn, the following evening. Several people are sitting at tables..."

Well, how many people? Where are the tables placed onstage? Is there a bar with stools? The scene culminates with all the men singing and dancing, "L'Chaim, To Life," so all the men should be in this number, but there can't be so many tables that they can't dance. A bar upstage with stools would help. Since the main dialogue is going to be between

Lazar and Tevye, it would probably be best to put Lazar's table down center. The men are all poor Jews in a tiny town in Russia.

There is little joy in their lives outside of their religious life, and these two factors draw them even closer to each other. And so they have an attitude and a relationship.

There are a few opening lines of dialogue, and the script says, "(Russians enter)." How many Russians? Three might be enough. Do the townspeople like the Russians? No. How would they react when the Russians enter? Do they move away? Do they talk quietly in dark corners? If the Russians are going to sit, is there an empty table for them, or do frightened townspeople stand and give their table to them? Later, as the men all sing and dance and the dance becomes quite lively, the Russians join them. What is their reaction? To stage the dance, do tables have to be moved? Who moves them?

Now here is a tough one. The following scene (Scene 5) is described as, "Street outside the inn. Entering from the inn door are Fiddler, Lazar Tevye, and others, singing 'To Life.'"

First of all, how is that scene change accomplished in ten seconds or less? Do we need to see the actual outside of the Inn? The scene is only a page and a half long. Do we need the door? Can we merely fly in a drop in front of the set and play this scene in front of the drop so the crew can be setting up Tevye's house for Scene 6? If so, how do we get the rest of the townspeople onstage so they can sing as they exit?

When the Russian Constable enters, how do the people react? Do they stop singing and laughing? Where and how do they exit?

The men in the chorus and the principals had all learned the song and they had all been choreographed in the number. They could sing it and they could dance it. But the scene doesn't come to life until they play the circumstances. So, making this scene work means my directing it so that everyone knows what it is about and what their function is.

Out of this example comes one of my fundamentals about integrating the chorus into the show: *Always play the circumstances.*

The chorus creates the environment of the show. It tells the audience where we are and how we should feel. The principals may have most of the dialogue, but it is the chorus that tells us this is a street in Hollywood, or this is an inn in Russia, or this is an island in the South Pacific.

Scenery and costumes help with location, but the ways the chorus act and interact tell a great deal about the environment. As an example, let's say there is a bare stage and the chorus enters. Tevye's friends and neighbors in *Fiddler* would behave much differently than the sailors and nurses in *South Pacific.* No matter what the location, we can tell a lot about their existence, what their lives are like, by they way in which they conduct themselves and interact. *Play the circumstances.*

The chorus also helps augment the mood of the show. My friend Morrie Enders uses an example to illustrate this point: "If Dolly Levi (in *Hello, Dolly!*) is happy to be back in Harmonia Gardens, that happiness is bigger when twenty waiters are ecstatic that she's back." That song and dance number grows from Dolly, singing by herself, expressing her happiness, to a huge love fest when the waiters are added. By the end of the number the audience is thrilled she is back.

The same thing happens in *Fiddler on the Roof.* Tevye and Lazar have agreed to the match and they begin with a toast. They are both very happy. As they start to sing their toasts, the chorus immediately joins in. Happy singing makes Tevye and Lazar's happiness even greater. Even the Russians join in singing, *"To your health and may we live together in peace."* Everyone dances to a wild finale and falls, exhausted, to the floor.

One caution: in scenes where there is a lot of dialogue and there are a lot of people onstage—principals and chorus—it is important that the director controls the focus. As directors we need to make sure the audience sees and hears what we want them to see and hear. Too much movement from chorus people will destroy focus. They need to listen and react appropriately, but in a way that they do not pull focus. An example: a principal has a very funny line and the chorus laughs. If one of the chorus members takes that laugh beyond what everyone else is doing, he will bring focus on himself and away from the principals. He needs to be told that this scene is not about him laughing. Usually, the chorus in a community theatre production is composed of the less-skilled, so they need to be told these things.

Somewhere along in this process of "putting it all together" I need to add in *all* of the music. If I'm using a pre-recorded orchestra, the cast has probably heard most of the music, but there are interludes and song lead-ups and underscoring that need to be brought into the last few rehearsals. I try to make time to do this before our first time onstage with a full orchestra. It can really throw actors for a loop to suddenly have some music playing while they are doing dialogue. They also need to know what words in their dialogue act as a cue for the conductor to start the lead-up to the song. (Those lines of dialogue are actually written into the conductor's music score.) If possible, I have the musical director/conductor bring in the entire orchestra to play for the last two or three rehearsals. That way, when we go onstage for our first technical rehearsals, we do not have to deal with music issues (except maybe "vamp 'til ready").

AFTERWORD

IF IT AIN'T FUN, IT AIN'T WORTH IT

My motto has always been, "If it ain't fun, it ain't worth it." Producing theatre is hard work. It can be tiring and exhausting because it requires one to draw on all the talent, skill, and imagination one possesses. For the actors it means hours of study and long, arduous rehearsals. For the designers and technicians it means many hours in the shop preparing, building, painting, gathering, and sewing. So why do we do this? We certainly don't do it for the money.

We do theatre because it's fun. Fun is a very important ingredient in any community theatre production. So what's fun about it? For most community theatre people, it means the opportunity to do something that they would not get to do in their everyday lives; it means learning new skills; it means developing a talent they never knew they had; it means producing a piece of art. I have always said that the production of a community theatre play is an amazing process. We gather together a group of people, many of whom do not know each other, many of whom have no theatrical experience, and in the course of a few weeks of rehearsal we produce a piece of art of good enough quality to be viewed by an audience.

Amazing!

Don't misunderstand me when I talk about fun. I don't mean "fun and games." I don't mean laughing and joking and having a "great old time." I mean the pure joy that comes from doing the best work you can through hard work. At the end of a long, exhausting rehearsal, everyone should feel wonderful about what they have accomplished that night, whether it's understanding a scene or learning a song or a new dance routine.

As directors we are in control of the "fun" element of producing theatre. We set the tone for all of the rehearsals. For me this means many things: when I'm directing a comedy, I like to keep the mood of rehearsals light and upbeat even though we are giving our full effort to make the comedy work; when I'm doing a drama, I try to set a more serious tone to encourage more thoughtful work from the actors. Positive reinforcement of an actor's efforts can have a great effect on his/her progress and increase the "fun" factor.

I have known directors who yell and scream at actors. I even know a director that threw an ashtray at an actor. To me, those directors are just putting on a show for their actors. Their egos are more important than the production. Abuse has no place in directing community theatre. Remember, these are community volunteers who are doing this for the fun of it.

GIVE 'EM YOUR BEST

Give 'Em Your Best is the theme of my opening night remarks to my casts and crews. Those people have a limited number of times they will get to perform the current production. When the run of the show is over, they might never have the opportunity to do it again. Therefore, I encourage them to give their best performance every night, with a note to each and every member of the company: "Give 'em your best." And I can think of no better advice with which to conclude here...no better advice to all aspiring actors and directors, stage hands and designers...all those connected with community theatre...no matter how large or small...no matter what goes wrong or goes right...no matter the makeup of the audience...this may be the only time it goes around...give 'em your best.

COMMUNITY THEATRE: OUR NATIONAL THEATRE

I have stressed for many years that community theatre is our "national theatre." Many countries around the world have important theatres that have been designated as their "national theatre."

We in the United States, have never put that title on any theatre. But consider this: more people attend community theatre productions than all of Broadway and Off-Broadway. Most people's first theatre experience as an adult is in a community theatre. At any one time, there are more community volunteers working on a production than professionals. And there is a "branch" of our national theatre in nearly every community.

REFERENCES

PLAYS QUOTED FROM OR REFERRED TO

By Neil Simon

BAREFOOT IN THE PARK
BRIGHTON BEACH MEMOIRS
LOST IN YONKERS
BILOXI BLUES
CHAPTER TWO
THE ODD COUPLE

By Henrik Ibsen

A DOLL'S HOUSE
THE MASTER BUILDER
AN ENEMY OF THE PEOPLE

By Moli'ere

THE IMAGINARY INVALID
THE DOCTOR IN SPITE OF HIMSELF
THE MISANTHROPE
THE MISER
TARTUFFE

By George Bernard Shaw

ARMS AND THE MAN
DON JUAN IN HELL
GETTING MARRIED
MAJOR BARBARA
YOU NEVER CAN TELL
PYGMALION

By Michael Frayne

NOISES OFF
THE FOREIGNER

By William Shakespeare

MACBETH
ROMEO AND JULIET

By Ray Cooney   RUN FOR YOUR WIFE
MOVE OVER, MRS. MARKHAM
TWO INTO ONE

DEATH OF A SALESMAN By Arthur Miller

PRIVATE LIVES By Noel Coward

ANNA CHRISTIE By Eugene O'Neill

NO SEX PLEASE, WE'RE BRITISH By Anthony Marriot and Alistar Foot

IN ONE BED...AND OUT THE OTHER By Mawby Green and Ed Feilbert

THE IMPORTANCE OF BEING EARNEST By Oscar Wilde

LEND ME A TENOR By Ken Ludwig

SUGAR BABIES By Ralph Allen and Harry Rigby

GREATER TUNA By Jason Williams, Joe Sears, and Ed Howard

SQUABBLES By Marshall Karp

WIT By Margaret Edson

A FEW GOOD MEN By Aaron Sorkin

TEAHOUSE OF THE AUGUST MOON By John Patrick

DRIVING MISS DAISY By Alfred Uhry

WHO'S AFRAID OF VIRGINIA WOOLF? By Edward Albee

STEEL MAGNOLIAS By Robert Harling

DANCING AT LUGHNASA By Brian Friel

THREE VIEWINGS By Jeffrey Hatcher

OVER THE RIVER AND THROUGH THE WOODS By Joe DiPietro

NIGHT MUST FALL By Emlyn Williams

AMADEUS By Peter Shaffer

TO KILL A MOCKINGBIRD By Christopher Sergel

THE FOURSOME By Norm Foster

THE ROYAL FAMILY By George S. Kaufman and Edna Ferber

I HATE HAMLET By Paul Rudnick

TUESDAYS WITH MORRIE By Mitch Albom

A CHORUS LINE By James Kirkwood, Nicholas Dante, Marvin Ham-
lisch, and Edward Kleban

42ND STREET By Michael Stewart, Mark Bram ble, Harry Warren, and
Al Dubin

ANYTHING GOES By Guy Betton, P.G. Wodehouse, Howard Lindsey,
Russel Crouse, and Cole Porter

SINGIN' IN THE RAIN By Betty Comden, Adolf Green, Arthur Freed,
and Nacio Herb Brown

OKLAHOMA! By Richard Rodgers and Oscar Hammerstein

LES MISERABLES By Alain Bloublil, Claude - Michel Schonberg, and
Herbert Kretzner

MISS SAIGON By Claude-Michel Schonberg and Alain Boublil

FIDDLER ON THE ROOF By Joseph Stein, Jerry Bock, and Sheldon Harnick

THE PRODUCERS By Mel Brooks and Thomas Meehan

MAMA MIA B y Cathe rine John son, Benn y An derson, and Bjorn Ulvaeus

PHANTOM OF THE OPERA By Andrew Lloyd Webber, Charles Hart, and Richard Stilgoe

CITY OF ANGELS By Cy Coleman

MY FAIR LADY By Alan Jay Lerner and Frederick Loewe

SOUTH PACIFIC By Richard Rodgers, Oscar Hammerstein, and Joshua Logan

HELLO, DOLLY! By Jerry Herman and Michael Stewart

A FUNNY THING HAPPENED ON THE WAY TO THE FORUM By Stephen Sondheim, Burt Shrevelove, and Larry Gelbart

JESUS CHRIST SUPERSTAR By Tim Rice and Andrew Lloyd Webber

WEST SIDE STOR Y By Arth ur Laurents, L eonard Bern stein, and Stephen Sondheim

THE BEST LITTLE WHOREHOUSE IN TEXAS By Larry King, Peter Masterson, and Carol Hall

BOOKS QUOTED FROM OR REFERRED TO

TIPS. Ideas For Directors. by Jon Jory

ON DIRECTING By Harold Cluman

FUNDAMENTALS OF PLAY DIIRECTING By Alexander Dean and
Lawrence Carra

NOTES

NOTES

NOTES

CPSIA information can be obtained at www.ICGtesting.com
Printed in the USA
BVOW020003230712

295833BV00001B/41/P